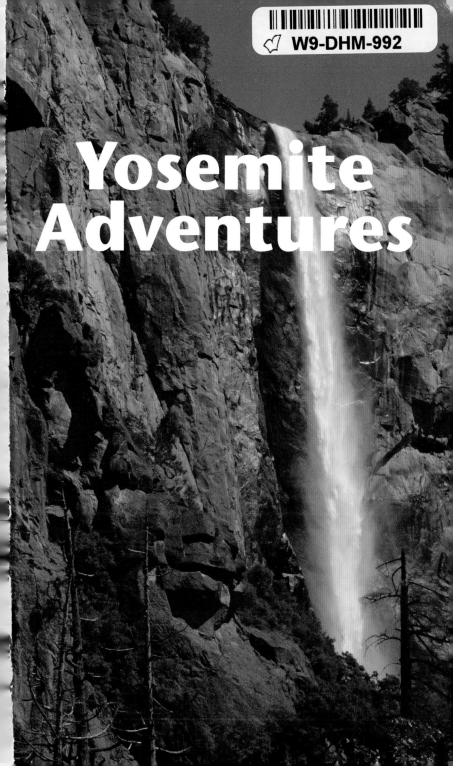

Yosemite Adventures

Yosemite Adventures

50 Spectacular Hikes, Climbs, and Winter Treks

Matt Johanson

TRIUMPH
BOOKS

Library of Congress Cataloging-in-Publication Data has been applied for.

This book is available in quantity at special discounts for your group or organization. For further information, contact:

Triumph Books LLC
814 North Franklin Street
Chicago, Illinois 60610
(312) 337-0747
www.triumphbooks.com

Printed in U.S.A.
ISBN: 978-1-60078-914-4
Design by Patricia Frey
Cover photo courtesy of Dan Johanson
Photos courtesy of the author except where otherwise noted

To the skilled and brave members of Yosemite Search and Rescue, with thanks for their tireless efforts to keep visitors safe, and to all who protect the park and share it with others

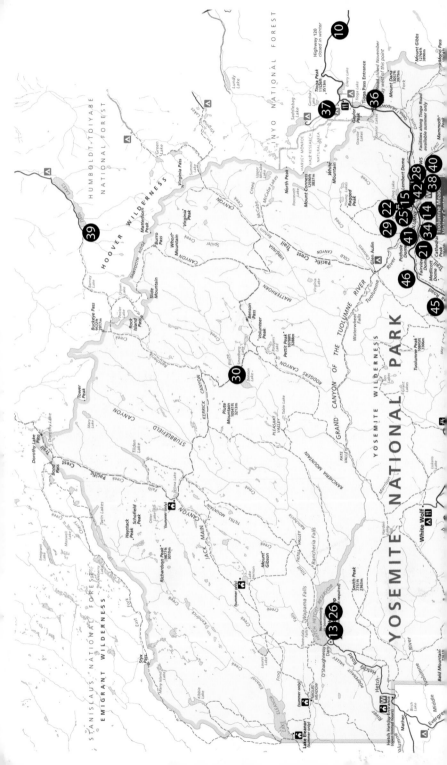

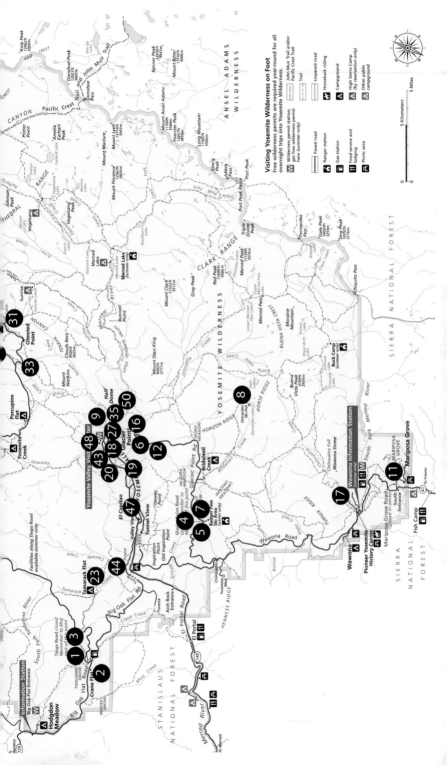

Contents

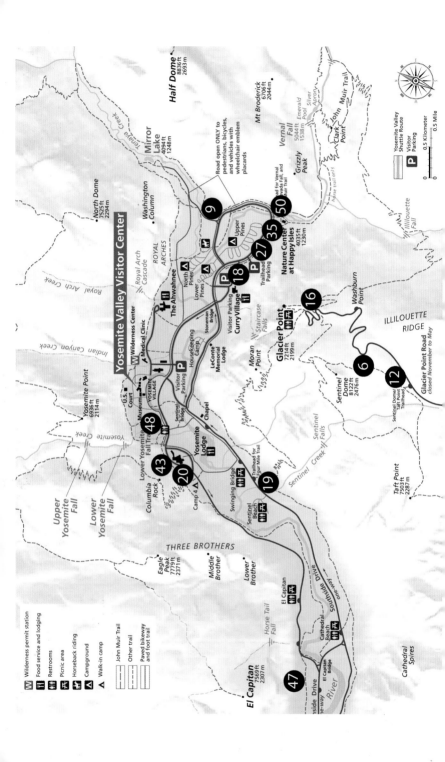

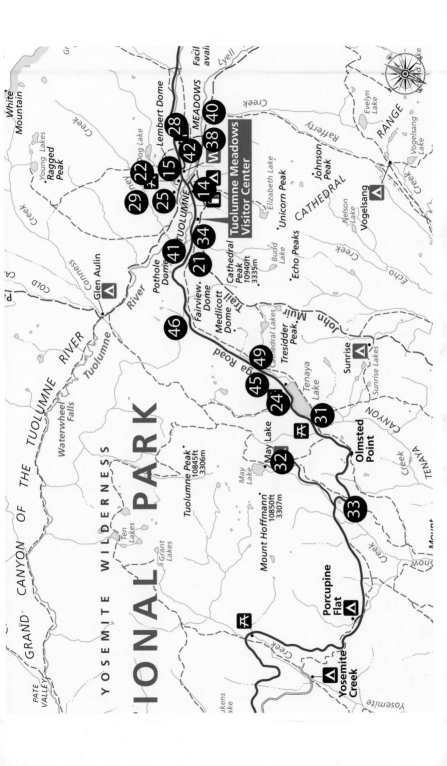

Foreword

You might take this as a local's bias, but many will agree with me that the following is true: the average outing in Yosemite is better than the best at any other area. Although Matt Johanson has some of the best in this book, he also has listed some of the less-frequented places. As a 30-year user of the park, I am eager to go explore these hikes and climbs. Surprisingly, many of them I haven't yet done.

There is a wealth of knowledge in this book for the adventurer wanting to hit some classic hikes, climbing routes, and winter treks. What's incredible is that there is no pretense that these outings listed are a "best of the best," or by any means a complete listing. They are not the hardest or the easiest. I do suspect that because many locals and guidebook authors are "spoiled" by Yosemite, these adventures listed herein may well be some of the forgotten gems. As a climber I get sucked into sticking to the technical routes Yosemite has to offer. Reading through some of the less technical peaks Matt has listed, I realize I am missing out on some fun mountaintop adventures. I will certainly have bagged some of them by the time you read this.

Just seeing the horizon full of peaks and cliffs can be overwhelming in a place like Yosemite. Matt gives you a nice manageable list of adventures to choose from.

I have to confess that my favorite climb in this book is Pine Line at the base of El Capitan. I've told many people that if you take the time to go do this rather simple 1-pitch route, you can say "I've climbed [on] El Capitan!" You can choose to leave out the "on." Just walking to the base of this route should be on everyone's short hike tick list. It's amazing to me how many people go to El Capitan Meadow and look up at El Cap, but how few take the 15-minute hike to go and place one's hand on the base of this 3,000-foot wall. Nowhere else in the world is this possible. But then that is true of the views from many of these adventures Matt has described.

Know that you are in good hands letting Matt choose some great paths for you to take on your next visit. Consider you may even run into a 30-year veteran of the park when you are out on any one of these gems. Hope I see you out there.

—Hans Florine

Hans Florine has won nine national climbing championships, authored Speed Climbing: How to Climb Faster and Better, *and set multiple speed climbing records, including the fastest-ever ascent of* The Nose of El Capitan in 2 hours, 23 minutes, and 46 seconds.

A snowy Lembert Dome welcomes winter visitors. Photo by Richard DeYoung

Winter Treks

Introduction to Winter Treks

Yosemite in winter sees just a fraction of the park's summer crowds while its snow-covered scenery becomes perhaps even grander. In addition to its rewards, the season provides unique challenges, especially during and after snowstorms. The following general tips will help adventurers enjoy the winter season safely.

Though it may sound oxymoronic, try to avoid snowy weather. Trekking around the mountains in a heavy winter storm is a trying experience which appeals to only a hardy few. Even driving to and from Yosemite in bad weather is difficult and dangerous, especially for those not accustomed to icy roads. Rescheduling a trip is often a better choice than pushing on through difficult conditions. Check the forecast and time your trip wisely.

When driving to and from Yosemite in winter, always carry chains and know how to put them on and remove them.

Most of the treks described in this book use trails that are marked (with markers on trees) but ungroomed. This means skiers and snowshoers will break trail through snow after every storm, and the first ones to arrive will do the hardest work. If this sounds daunting, simply plan your visit for a week or more after heavy snow. By this time, others will probably have broken trail ahead of you, making traveling and staying on route much easier.

Most Yosemite winter trekkers use snowshoes, which offer easy use. Cross-country skis require more skill but permit travel that's faster, easier, and more fun. Skis with metal edges and heavy bindings are the best choice for backcountry trips involving trail breaking and steep climbs and descents. Beginners may want to experiment with several options by renting before buying gear.

A word about avalanches is in order. The trips described in this book generally avoid avalanche hazards, but those who brave the backcountry in winter should develop awareness of them. For starters, avoid steep terrain (from 30 to 50 degrees) during heavy snow and for a few days afterward. Avoid crossing steep slopes, especially those that face south and in the afternoon. Travel with at least one partner and a snow shovel.

Dress for success. This means using layers and wearing materials like wool, which insulate temperature even when wet, and avoiding cotton, which does not.

Even in winter, prepare for the sun. In fact, the sunshine reflected off snow at high elevation may be the most intense you will ever experience. Bring a wide-brimmed hat, sunglasses, and sunscreen.

Photo by Dan Johanson

Finally, hope for the best and plan for the worst. This advice applies particularly well to winter outings in Yosemite. In particular, those attempting to reach ski cabins or even taking long day trips should prepare to camp overnight in case it becomes needed. Pack accordingly.

Please bury human waste and pack out toilet paper. Overnight travelers are required to obtain a wilderness permit.

Recommended gear:

skis or snowshoes
boots
poles
gaiters
gloves
ski hat
water bottles
map
compass
snow shovel
sunglasses (spares are also advised)
sunscreen (the stronger the better)
ski wax
first aid kit

For overnight trips, bring:

warm sleeping bag
inflatable mattress
tent or bivvy sack
stove with fuel
matches and/or lighter
mess kit
headlamp or flashlight
toilet paper

Optional items:

camera
GPS device
snow slippers
for skiers, climbing skins (these adhesive-coated fabric strips make skiing
uphill much easier in icy conditions and are essential on many backcountry
ski treks)

Author's journal of trans-Sierra ski trek, 2002:

As we gazed over Tuolumne Meadows and countless snowy pinnacles, we saw not a soul and scarcely a sign that people had ever been there. It was hard to believe we were in one of the world's most popular parks, visited by millions every year. To reach the 9,450-foot summit of Lembert Dome in summer involves an easy hike, but to earn that view in winter we had to ski for two days and then trudge upwards through deep powder. Cliff, Richard, and I carefully hiked the final steps over rock and ice to reach a patch of bare granite. The amazing view from the peak was our reward.

Tuolumne Grove
of Giant Sequoias

Distance: 2 miles round trip
Time: 1 to 3 hours
Difficulty: easy
Parking and trailhead: Tuolumne Grove, elevation 6,200 feet
Highest point: elevation 6,200 feet
Best season: January through April
Permits: none needed

Overview

Here's a great first winter outing for beginning skiers and snowshoers. A gentle path leads to dozens of beautiful giant sequoias. From the parking area, go north past the restrooms and gate and down a forest road. The first sequoias come into view after a sharp turn. A side trail leads to the tunnel tree and then reconnects with the main path. Be prepared to hike uphill on the way back. This is also a fine trip in spring, summer, and fall.

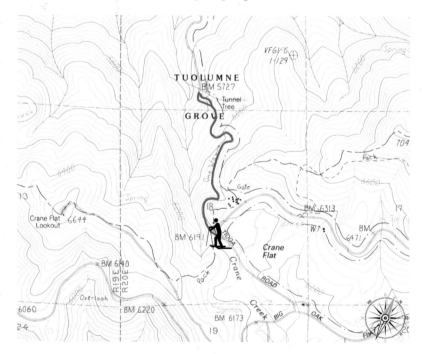

Crane Flat

Distance: 3 miles round trip
Time: 2 to 4 hours
Difficulty: easy
Parking and trailhead: Crane Flat Lookout turnoff from Big Oak Flat Road (just west of Crane Flat Campground), elevation 6,250 feet
Summit: elevation 6,645 feet
Best season: January through April
Permits: none needed

Overview

An enjoyable trek leads to the most scenic winter vista that's easily accessible in the park. Crane Flat delivers a panoramic view and a good look at the Clark Range. From the turnoff, pass the gate and follow the forest road to the northwest. After taking in the scenery, enjoy downhill all the way back. Once a fire lookout, Crane Flat still serves as a search and rescue base.

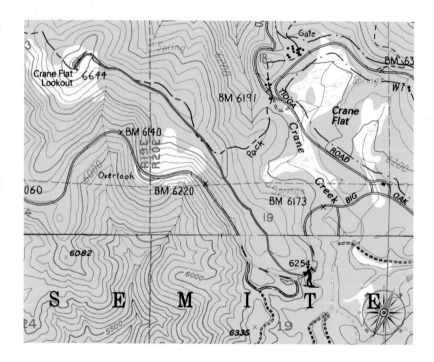

Clark Range seen from Crane Flat

3 Gin Flat Loop

Distance: 6 miles
Time: 2 to 4 hours
Difficulty: moderate
Parking: Tuolumne Grove lot
Trailhead: Tioga Road gate near Crane Flat, elevation 6,200 feet
Highest point: elevation 7,100 feet
Best season: January through April
Permits: none needed

Overview

This outing provides a medium-sized adventure on a forest loop. From the Tuolumne Grove lot, walk east on Tioga Road beside Crane Flat Meadow and past the winter gate. Continue a quarter mile until the loop splits. Turn left onto Gin Flat Trail. Your path turns and climbs up a hillside for a few miles to Gin Flat. Turn right onto Tioga Road to return to your start.

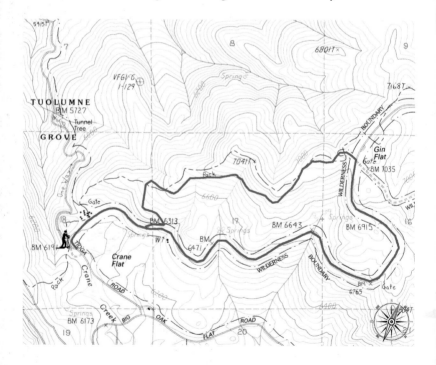

Dewey Point Loop

Distance: 7 miles
Time: 4 to 6 hours
Difficulty: easy to moderate
Parking and trailhead: Badger Pass Ski Area, elevation 7,216 feet
Highest point: elevation 7,560 feet
Best season: January through March
Permits: none needed for day use but required for overnight travel; visit the Badger Pass A-frame rangers' office

Overview

A marked, well-traveled trail leads to a spectacular viewpoint and an especially good view of El Capitan. The gentle route meanders through a peaceful meadow and forest before descending to the valley rim where visitors can see deep into the snow-capped backcountry. Return the same way or take a more challenging ridge variation back instead. This is a must for Yosemite winter enthusiasts.

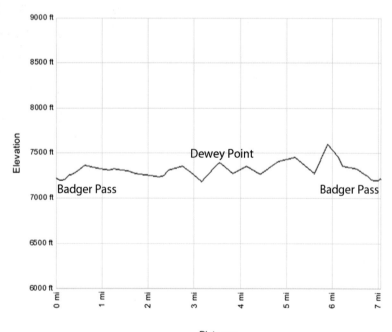

El Capitan seen from Dewey Point

Skiing the ski trek

Start east on the often-groomed Glacier Point Road, climbing gently and then descending at Summit Meadow. About a mile from the parking lot, look for the signed Dewey Point Meadow Trail (#18) on your left, breaking from the road and heading north. The next mile is easy going through the flat meadow along a creek and framed by lodgepole pines.

Then the trail drops, curves, and becomes more difficult, joining with the Dewey Point Ridge Trail as it passes through denser trees before emerging for a final climb to the rim and viewpoint at 7,385 feet. You'll feel like you're looking off the edge of the world. Spend some time here admiring The Captain, the Cathedral Rocks, and other landmarks.

When you're ready to return, you have a choice of routes. If the trip out challenged you, then it's best to return the same way. But if you're ready for some variety, a few hills, and a more rigorous segment, then you might try the Dewey Point Ridge Trail (#14). To choose this option, retrace your steps about a mile to the signed trail junction and turn right up the hill. The signed route rolls up and down like a roller coaster. As usual, skiers will get a bigger payoff on the downhills than snowshoers.

The trail connects with Glacier Point Road. Turn right toward the Badger Pass parking lot, less than a mile to the west.

Insider tips

Because skiers and snowshoers both frequent the Dewey Point Meadow Trail, it's important for each group to stay on their respective tracks. Snowshoes break up ski tracks by walking over them and put skiers at risk of falls and injuries.

Skiers should take skins for the steeper parts of the outing, especially if they intend to return on the Dewey Point Ridge Trail.

If you have time at Dewey Point, you may want to trace the rim west for a half-mile to reach Crocker Point or a mile to reach Stanford Point.

Consider spending a night here. The sunset and sunrise are incomparable.

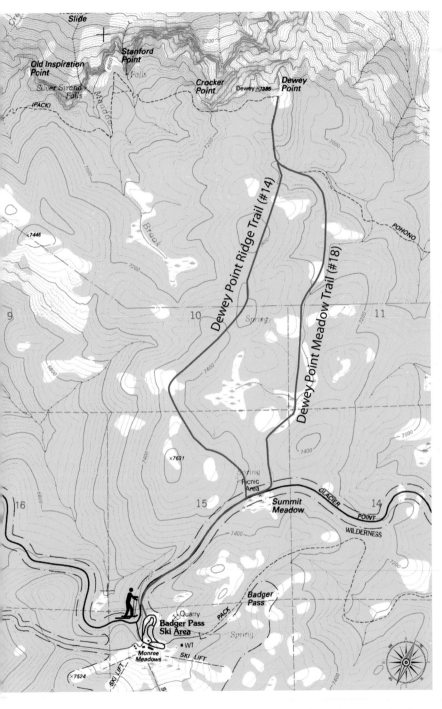

Glacier Point

Distance: 21 miles round trip
Time: 2 days or more
Difficulty: moderate
Parking and trailhead: Badger Pass Ski Area (park in the overnight area near the back), elevation 7,216 feet
Highest point: elevation 7,868 feet
Best season: January through March
Permits: none needed for day use but required for overnight travel; visit the Badger Pass A-frame rangers' office

Overview

This trek provides a great introduction to overnight winter touring and camping. While the 10.5 mile distance from Badger Pass to Glacier Point requires commitment, the route along a paved road is often machine-groomed. Long, gentle slopes provide fun descents. Many trekkers camp near the rim. Those who desire a more upscale experience can reserve beds at the Glacier Point Ski Hut.

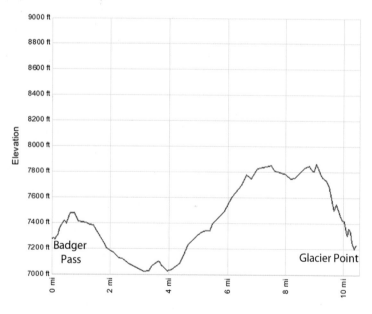

Half Dome seen from Glacier Point

Skiing the ski trek

While some speedsters make this round trip in a day, most enjoy a night or more at one of the Sierra Nevada's finest viewpoints. If you do so, your first decision is whether to camp or stay at Glacier Point Ski Hut. Camping is free and quite comfortable in good conditions for those properly equipped. Glacier Point Ski Hut provides its guests with bunk beds and hot meals for prices starting at $120 per night. Reservations are required; contact concessionaire Delaware North at (209) 372-8444 or through yosemitepark.com.

Your journey traces Glacier Point Road the entire way, so route finding should not be a problem. First the road climbs about a mile to Summit Meadow. Next comes a 2-mile drop to Bridalveil Creek Campground. After crossing Bridalveil Creek Bridge a half mile later, enjoy your last descent for a while. As you pass a sign for Horizon Ridge Trail, you'll begin a 3-mile climb that gains about 800 feet. During this segment on clear days, you will get a fantastic view of the Clark Range, an impressive series of peaks to the east. The route flattens in the final miles as it passes Sentinel Dome to the northwest. Then descend on the road's switchbacks as you pass an awesome Half Dome vista and arrive at Glacier Point.

Be forewarned, a visit to snowbound Glacier Point may instill a lifelong love of winter adventure.

Insider tips

Park workers use a snowcat to groom snow on Glacier Point Road, but do not do so every day. A storm that strikes while you are out may require you to break miles of trail on a return trip! Watch the weather forecast.

Because of its long slopes and the often-groomed snow, this trek is especially suited to skis rather than snowshoes.

Distances and details

Start: Badger Pass
3.2 miles: Bridalveil Creek Campground
3.6 miles: Bridalveil Creek Bridge
4.9 miles: Horizon Ridge Trailhead (stay on road)
6.1 miles: Clark Range view
8.9 miles: Sentinel Dome parking area
9.2 miles: Top of hill before switchbacks
10.5 miles: Glacier Point
21 miles: Return to Badger Pass

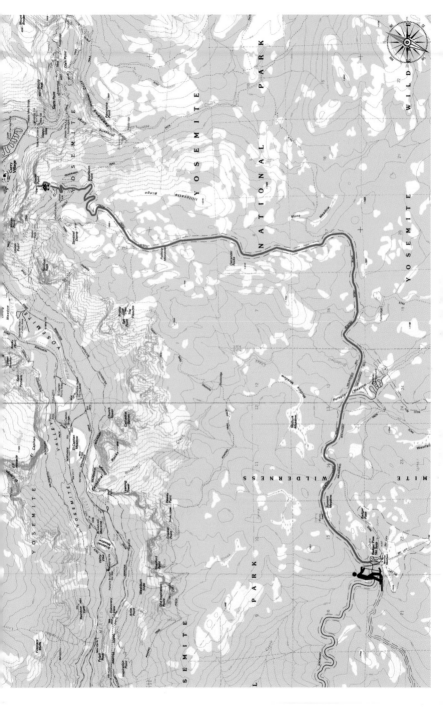

Glacier Point Side Trip: Sentinel Dome

Distance: 1 mile round trip
Time: 1 hour
Difficulty: easy
Starting point: Glacier Point Road above switchbacks descent to Glacier Point (about 0.75 miles west of summer parking area); elevation 7,700 feet
Summit: elevation 8,122 feet
Best season: January through March
Permits: none needed for day use but required for overnight travel; visit the Badger Pass A-frame rangers' office

Overview

Here's an easy climb to a great outlook higher than Glacier Point. The winter route is different from the summer trail. Traveling east on Glacier Point Road, pass the Sentinel Dome/Taft Point Trailhead and restroom. About three quarters of a mile farther, the road turns sharply right. Instead, go straight (west) to climb to a saddle south of the dome. Climb counterclockwise to the north to the summit.

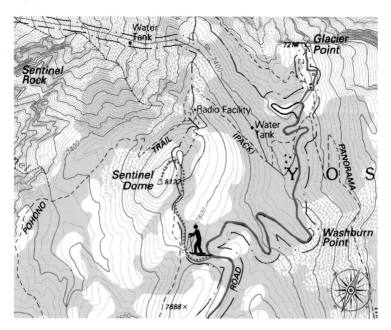

Yosemite Falls seen from Sentinel Dome

7 Ostrander Ski Hut

Distance: 18 miles round trip
Time: 2 days or more
Difficulty: strenuous
Parking and trailhead: Badger Pass Ski Area (park in the overnight area near the back); elevation 7,216 feet
Ostrander Hut: elevation 8,527 feet
Best season: January through March (Ostrander usually opens after Christmas and closes in early April; check with the Yosemite Conservancy)
Permits: required for overnight travel; visit the Badger Pass A-frame rangers' office

Overview

Ostrander has sheltered winter travelers since 1941. Built by President Roosevelt's Civilian Conservation Corps, the hut has bunk beds, a wood stove, firewood, a small kitchen, tables, benches, lights, and toilets. What Ostrander lacks in privacy, it makes up in charm. Rookies, beware: the 9-mile trek from Badger Pass to Ostrander can be anything from comfortable to horrendous, depending on ability, gear, snow conditions, and weather.

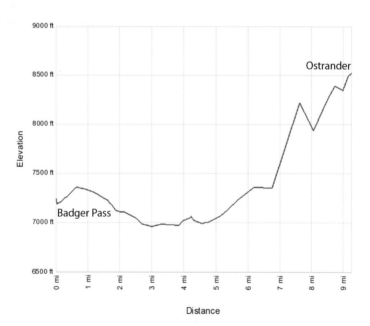

Skiing the ski trek

Do this trip right and you'll see why many skiers return to Ostrander every year. The rustic cabin feels like a world unto itself, an oasis of comfort and cheer in a winter wonderland. Yet many have underestimated the journey and spent freezing nights outdoors as a result. Prepare carefully!

Ostrander-bound skiers should be in good shape and comfortable exercising at 8,000 feet. Use backcountry skis with sharp metal edges and boots with strong bindings; track skis do not cut it where you're going. Snowshoes are another option, slower but easier for backcountry beginners.

The cabin books up months in advance so reservations are a good idea. Visit yosemiteconservancy.org for reservation information. Overnight use fees run up to $50, with discounts for midweek visitors and youths.

Hitting the trail by 9:00 AM is a good idea. Horizon Ridge Ski Trail is the easiest route. For 5 miles, you'll enjoy groomed ski tracks along Glacier Point Road, mostly downhill in the outbound direction. After Bridalveil Creek, watch for the sign to turn right onto the signed trail (#15). Reflective trail markers nailed to trees mark the route from here. Now the fun begins and you'll gain about a thousand feet climbing Heart Attack Hill, but a warm cabin awaits beside Ostrander Lake.

High-quality cooking is an Ostrander tradition. Upgrade your usual backcountry fare if you don't want to be outclassed!

Insider tips

Ostrander Hut is located at latitude 37°37.60' N, longitude 119°32.99' W.

Prepare for a night in the snow, just in case. Bring a sleeping bag, air mattress, tent/bivvy sack, stove, and pot.

Ostrander may have same-day availability, even on weekends. Inquire before departing at the Badger Pass A-frame rangers' office.

Plan at least a three-day trip. After a hard effort to reach Ostrander, you deserve a day to rest and enjoy the cabin and surroundings before heading back.

At 10.3 miles, the Bridalveil Creek Trail is slightly longer and comparable in difficulty. The Merced Crest route is 9.7 miles and highly scenic but far more difficult.

Distances and details

Start: Badger Pass
3.6 miles: Bridalveil Creek Bridge
4.9 miles: Horizon Ridge Trailhead (turn right)
9 miles: Ostrander Hut
18 miles: Return to Badger Pass

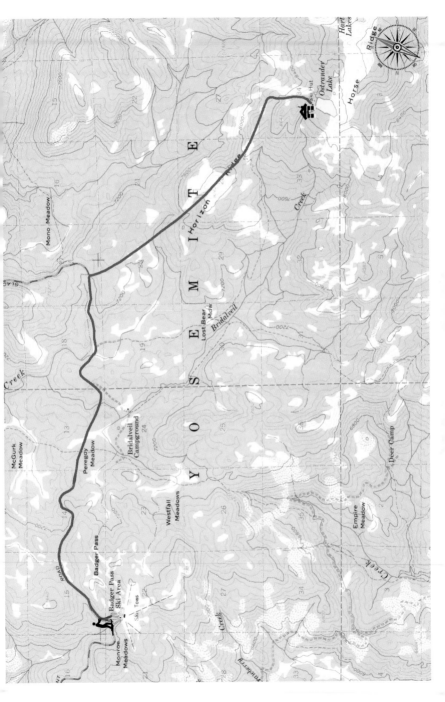

8 Ostrander Side Trip: Buena Vista Peak

Distance: 8 miles round trip
Time: 4 to 6 hours
Difficulty: strenuous
Starting point: Ostrander Ski Hut, elevation 8,527 feet
Buena Vista Peak: elevation 9,709 feet
Best season: January through March
Permits: required for overnight travelers; visit the Badger Pass A-frame rangers' office

Overview

Reaching Ostrander Ski Hut feels good, but using the cabin as a base for deeper wilderness experiences feels great. In the right conditions, Buena Vista Peak provides just such an outing. This is the most appealing alpine summit within striking distance of the hut. No marked trail leads all the way from Ostrander to Buena Vista Peak and skiers need experience in route finding and avalanche safety.

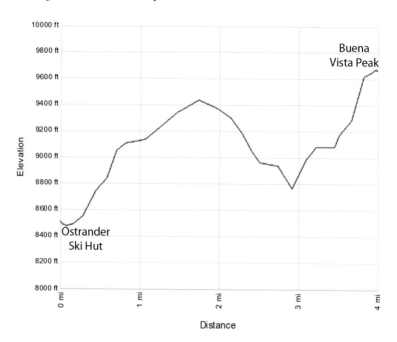

Andy Padlo nears the summit of Buena Vista Peak.

Skiing the ski trek

First let's make sure you want to do this. Those who would summit Buena Vista Peak in winter should be fit and experienced backcountry skiers, familiar with route finding, skiing off marked trails, and able to spot and avoid avalanche hazards. They should be equipped with backcountry skis, skins, map and compass, food, water, and suitable clothes. They should make the outing a week or more after heavy snow, letting powder settle for easier skiing and minimal avalanche danger. And they should attempt this outing only with one or more partners, not alone.

Still want to go? Good! From the hut, pick up signed trail #17, which curves counterclockwise around the west end of Horse Ridge. There may be gaps in the signs but the route traces the south face of the ridge from the west to the east, climbing to the crest before dropping southeast toward a prominent saddle, where the signed trail ends.

From the saddle, ski southeast toward Buena Vista Lake. Some skiers cross the frozen surface in deep winter; judge conditions for yourself and if in doubt, go around. Climb up the north face, making a clockwise curve to reach the northeast ridge, and climb southwest to the peak.

Savor the summit view and return safely to share the story with your hutmates around the Ostrander dinner table.

Insider tips

Make this trip on a clear day. The summit will be harder to reach and enjoy if low clouds obscure your view.

The south face of Buena Vista Peak is known for great slopes and snow; it's worth a run if you have the time.

Be careful on the return to the cabin. Some have missed their western turn toward Horse Ridge, gone too far north toward Mount Starr King, and were "nighted" (forced to spend the night outdoors) as a result.

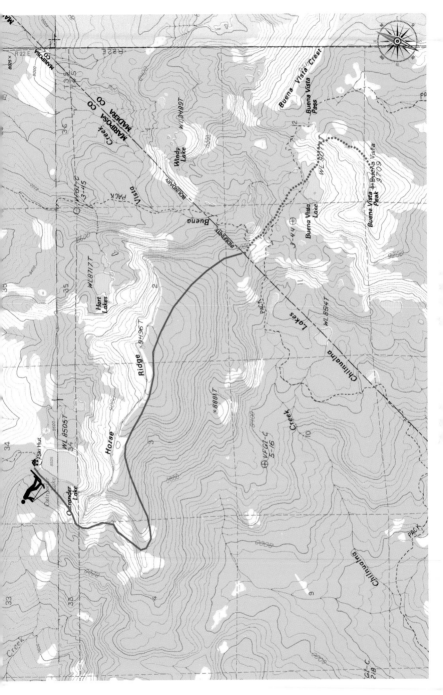

Snow Creek Cabin

Distance: 12.2 miles round trip
Time: 2 days or more
Difficulty: strenuous
Parking: trailhead parking area (southwest of road between Curry Village and Happy Isles)
Trailhead: Mirror Lake bus stop, elevation 4,000 feet
Snow Creek Cabin: elevation 7,740 feet
Best season: January through March
Permits: required for overnight travel; visit Yosemite Valley Visitor Center

Overview

Built in 1929 but long in disrepair and closed, Snow Creek Cabin reopened in 2006 thanks to the gallant effort of volunteers. Climbing 3,740 feet up Snow Creek Trail requires a high level of fitness and determination, but those who do so enjoy a superior view of Half Dome on the way and often privacy at the cabin when they arrive.

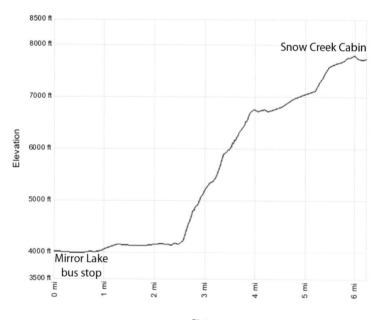

Skiing the ski trek

This gem stands at the crossroads between Yosemite Valley and Tuolumne Meadows, housing visitors from both directions. Open in winter only, Snow Creek Cabin has a stove, firewood, kitchen, tables, benches, lanterns, and an outhouse. It currently shelters visitors free of charge. Verify the cabin is open at the Yosemite Valley Visitor Center before departing.

Skiers and snowshoers should be in good shape with prior wilderness experience and route-finding skills. The elevation gain will be formidable and winter gear makes for a heavy backpack.

Take the shuttle to the Mirror Lake stop. Follow the road past Mirror Lake. Then join the trail leading northeast toward Tenaya Canyon. Walk beneath North Dome and Basket Dome before reaching a signed junction. Turn left onto Snow Creek Trail. Now the fun begins and you'll gain about 3,000 feet on switchbacks over 2 miles.

After leveling, the trail crosses a bridge over Snow Creek. More gradual climbing follows. Snow deepens here and you'll want to put on skis or snowshoes. Then a shorter set of switchbacks leads to a stream crossing (no bridge) and trail junction. Turn right (east) toward Olmsted Point.

About a third of a mile past the trail junction, cut south through the trees. There is no sign or marked trail, though there may be tracks to guide you. Past the trees in a meadow, look east toward Mount Watkins and you'll see the cabin through the trees. Treat it with care so the park will continue to make it available.

Insider tips

Snow Creek Cabin is located at latitude 37°46.43' N, longitude 119°32.36' W.

Enjoy nearby Mount Watkins before returning. From the cabin to the 8,500-foot summit is less than a mile and 750 feet of elevation gain.

Visitors can cache food prior to the Tioga Road closure. This requires a 5-mile round trip hike from Tioga Road. Use the lockers outside the cabin.

Distances and details

Start: Mirror Lake bus stop
1.0 miles: Mirror Lake
1.6 miles: Junction with Snow Creek Trail (turn left)
4.2 miles: Bridge over Snow Creek
5.8 miles: Trail junction (stay right)
6.1 miles: Snow Creek Cabin
12.2 miles: Return to Mirror Lake bus stop

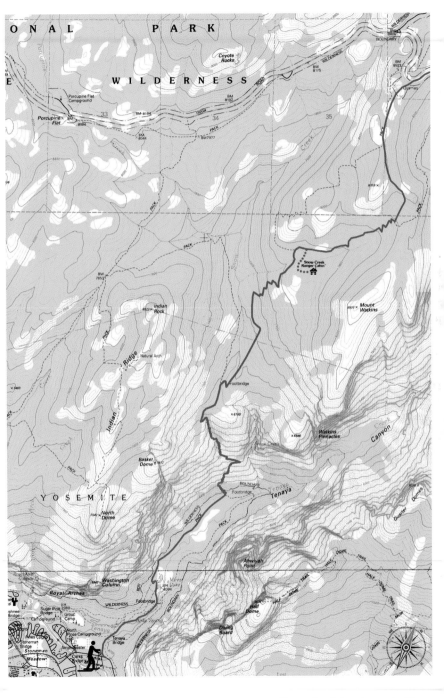

Trans-Sierra:
Lee Vining to Yosemite Valley

Distance: 39 miles
Time: 3 to 6 days
Difficulty: moderate (in good conditions)
Parking and trailhead: Lee Vining winter gate on Tioga Road/
Highway 120, elevation 7,400 feet
Tioga Pass: elevation 9,943 feet
Best season: February through April
Permits: required for overnight travel; visit the Forest Service Visitor
Center north of Lee Vining or Yosemite Valley Visitor Center

Overview

Journeying through Tuolumne Meadows in winter is a lifetime highlight
and this trek is more achievable than many people realize. Because it traces
Tioga Road, the route finding and skiing are basic in good conditions. The
route also features two public ski cabins that are available for free. Those
who manage the adventure are rewarded with a passage through some of
Yosemite's most spectacular high country.

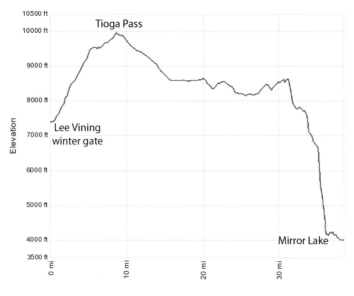

Animal tracks point to Tenaya Peak.

Skiing the ski trek

Several important decisions must precede an attempt of this coveted trans-Sierra trek. First, where to start and finish? This guide recommends traveling westbound beginning near the eastern Sierra town of Lee Vining (7,400 feet) and finishing in Yosemite Valley. This choice saves visitors 3,400 feet of climbing compared to the eastbound alternative and avoids a particularly difficult initial climb out of Yosemite Valley up Snow Creek Trail.

Second, skis or snowshoes? Even more than other Yosemite winter outings, this trip calls for skis. Covering 35 miles on snowshoes could require several additional days. In addition, the terrain is perfect for skiing, with long gentle slopes on either side of Tioga Pass and elsewhere.

Third, how to arrange transportation? Amtrak operates trains and buses from the west side of the mountains to Reno and the Eastern Sierra Transit Authority runs buses from Reno to Lee Vining. In recent years Alaska and United Airlines have flown between Mammoth (south of Lee Vining) and various Bay Area and Southern California airports. Many skiers drive and rely on kindly friends and relatives to assist with drop-offs and pick-ups.

Once you're ready to go in Lee Vining, drive west up Highway 120 about 3 miles to the winter gate closure. Here you strap on your pack and hit the road. You may be able to ski right away, though later in the season, you'll probably need to walk a few miles to reach the snowline. From the gate to Tioga Pass is about 9 miles, steadily climbing about 2,500 feet. You may wish to camp here after a hard day's work and enjoy the view.

Peaks of Lee Vining Canyon

The ambitious continue on to reach Tuolumne Ski Hut on the first night. From the pass, the route gently descends 1,400 feet over 7 miles before passing Lembert Done and crossing a bridge over the Tuolumne River. Here the hut stands south of the road. Inside are 10 bunk beds, available for free on a first-come, first-serve basis. The hut also has a wood stove, firewood, tables, lights, and an electric stove. Those who plan ahead can reap another benefit of this shelter. Behind the cabin stands a bear-proof storage bin where visitors can cache food in the fall before the road's winter closure.

The hut is seldom used in December, January, and February, but holds more visitors in March and April. Prepare to camp in case there's no space available.

If you've come this far, you really should schedule a day to linger here and enjoy the surroundings. Dog Dome and Lembert Dome are both pleasant outings from the hut. Skiing through Tuolumne Meadows without a heavy pack will liberate the body and spirit.

When continuing your westbound journey, start early for the best skiing. Late in the season, snow here will soften in the afternoon, making for a slow, slushy go. Pothole Dome, with gentle slopes and a nice summit view, is worth a short detour. About 8 miles from the hut, skiers reach picturesque Tenaya Lake, a perfect spot for lunch.

The route's main avalanche hazard is found on the next segment. Granite slopes prone to snow slides stand just short of Olmsted Point. Skiers are advised to avoid this area during and after heavy snowfall and on sunny afternoons. In any case, pass by it quickly.

Olmsted commands an awesome view of Tenaya Canyon and Half Dome. This would be a great place to camp, though pushing on 4 miles to Snow Creek Cabin is another option.

Continue west on Tioga Road about 1.6 miles until reaching a sharp bend to the right (maps will show a quarry south of the road). Here begins the trickiest route-finding of the trip because the trail leaves the paved road; see the Snow Creek Cabin map on page 47. There may be tracks to guide you (except during or after a storm) and it's not too complicated in any case with a map and compass. Follow a tree-marked winter trail southbound along the obvious ridge. The route will eventually descend, still southward, on the east side of the ridge before turning to the west.

Now you're just a mile from Snow Creek Cabin. At this writing, the shelter operates much like Tuolumne Hut: there is no charge and no guarantee of space. Inside are tables, benches, mattresses, a wood stove, and firewood. Outside are bear lockers in which hikers can store food for winter

Fairview Dome

use. To reach Snow Creek Cabin, ski about .75 miles from the westward turn and then head south. The cabin is about a quarter of a mile south of the marked trail in a woody meadow. Please treat it with care so the park will continue to make it available.

To complete your odyssey, pick up Snow Creek Trail heading south and descending. Cross a wooden bridge over Snow Creek in about 2 miles. Somewhere in this area the snow will become patchy and disappear. Take off your skis and be glad you have your poles to ease the steep descent into Yosemite Valley. After a formidable series of switchbacks, turn right toward Mirror Lake. Now you're in the homestretch. As you walk the last steps to the Mirror Lake bus stop, enjoy the awed looks of tourists in sandals staring at your pack and skis. If you want to really impress them, tell them you just skied trans-Sierra.

Insider tips

Tuolumne Ski Hut is located at latitude 37°46.43' N, longitude 119°32.36' W. During the fall, cache non-perishable food in the storage bin behind the hut (which doubles as a camping office in summer).

Snow Creek Cabin is located at latitude 37°46.43' N, longitude 119°32.36' W. It also has bear-proof food storage, though reaching this shelter before winter requires a 5-mile round-trip hike from Tioga Road.

Besides ski boots, take a pair of shoes for cabin use and the trek's beginning and end.

Distances and details

Start: Lee Vining winter gate
9 miles: Tioga Pass, park entrance
17 miles: Tuolumne Ski Hut
27.4 miles: Olmsted Point
29 miles: Winter route to Snow Creek
32 miles: Snow Creek Cabin
33.9 miles: Bridge over Snow Creek
36.5 miles: Junction with Mirror Lake Trail (turn right)
38 miles: Mirror Lake
39 miles: Mirror Lake bus stop

View from Glacier Point

Hiking

Introduction to Hiking

Want to experience breathtaking vistas and spectacular waterfalls? Looking for a short loop or an all-day adventure? When it comes to hiking, Yosemite truly has it all.

While there's almost no bad time to go hiking in Yosemite, spring and fall deserve special consideration. Heat and crowding can be formidable during the summer, especially in Yosemite Valley, and the high country will be snowed over in winter. But in the shoulder seasons, temperatures are pleasant and crowds are manageable. Waterfalls flow impressively in the spring. Mosquitoes disappear in the fall. Tioga Road and Glacier Point Road generally open in June.

Consider elevation when planning a trip. People coming from sea level will need to acclimate to the thinner mountain air, especially in high country areas like Tuolumne Meadows. Give yourself time and drink plenty of water.

Protect yourself from the sun with proper clothes and sunscreen. Those strolling happily on mountain trails in tank tops and without hats pay a heavy price in sunburn.

This guide strongly recommends the use of hiking poles on steep hikes, especially for those who have turned 40 or someday plan to do so. Stay on trails and do not take "short cuts."

Pets and bicycles are not permitted on trails. Please pack out all trash.

Permits are not required for day trips, with the exception of hikers summiting Half Dome; wilderness permits are required for overnight backcountry travel.

Wildflowers abound on Yosemite day hikes.

Recommended gear:
boots
hiking poles
water bottles
map
compass
sunglasses (spares are also advised)
sunscreen (the stronger the better)
first aid kit
water filter and/or iodine tablets

Optional items:
camera
GPS device
Mosquito netting and/or repellant

Author's journal of hiking the Yosemite Falls Trail, 1995:

Storm clouds threatened but we started the hike anyway. Up (and up and up) we climbed through icy rain and bone-chilling winds. The hike is one of the park's most popular outings but we had it to ourselves on a cold, blustery day. Several times we considered turning back but, wisely or not, pushed on to the viewing ledge. There we reveled in the awesome spectacle of roaring Upper Yosemite Fall before hustling back down to beat the storm. My brother Danny was 19 and I was 24 on our first Yosemite adventure together, which set the stage for many more.

Mariposa Grove of Giant Sequoias

Distance: 3.5 miles
Time: 2 to 3 hours
Difficulty: easy
Parking and trailhead: Mariposa Grove lot, elevation 5,600 feet
Highest point: elevation 6,427 feet
Best season: April through November
Permits: none needed

Overview

Giant sequoias are the largest and among the most beautiful trees on Earth. Mariposa Grove holds more than 500 giant sequoias, the largest cluster in Yosemite. This loop leads past the picturesque Grizzly Giant, Bachelor, Three Graces, and California Tunnel Tree.

Hiking the hike

Giant sequoias can live longer than 3,000 years. Walking amongst them feels like traveling back in time. It's a journey worth taking.

Fallen Monarch, a massive sequoia that fell centuries ago, first greets hikers on the main trail. Bachelor and Three Graces, a photogenic cluster, stand just beyond the road crossing. Keep moving to reach Grizzly Giant, one of the largest sequoias in the world, standing more than 200 feet tall. Beyond it is the California Tunnel Tree, which amazingly survived the attack of ax-wielding vandals in 1895.

Continue to the museum, where restrooms and water are available. Here starts an optional detour to the Upper Grove where more sequoias and Wawona Point Vista are found. Return downhill on the trail that passes Clothespin Tree and the Faithful Couple.

Most of these trees have stood since before the voyage of Columbus. Come meet your elders.

Insider tips

Arrive early to park in the main lot, which fills up on busy days, or take the free shuttle from Wawona.

Though the 2-mile road to the grove closes to traffic in winter, skiers can still trek there.

Grizzly Giant

Bachelor and Three Graces

Taft Point

Distance: 2.2 miles round trip
Time: 1 to 2 hours
Difficulty: easy
Parking and trailhead: Sentinel Dome/Taft Point Trailhead on Glacier Point Road; elevation 7,680 feet
Taft Point: elevation 7,503 feet
Best season: June through October
Permits: none needed

Overview

This hike through a pine forest delivers a dramatic look at El Capitan. Follow the signs west from the parking area. Look straight down 3,500 feet from behind a railing and marvel at the Taft Fissures. On the return, hikers can ascend Sentinel Dome and return to the trailhead on a signed loop that adds 3 miles.

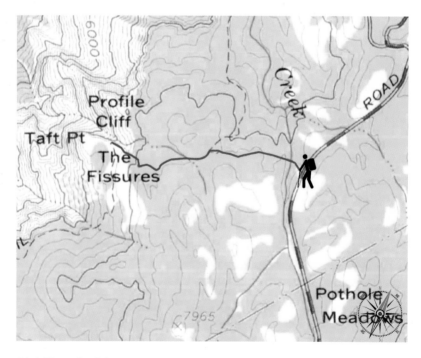

El Capitan seen from Taft Point

Wapama Falls

Distance: 5 miles round trip
Time: 2 to 4 hours
Difficulty: easy
Parking: lot beside O'Shaughnessy Dam at Hetch Hetchy Reservoir
Trailhead: O'Shaughnessy Dam, 3,820 feet
Wapama Falls: elevation 4,050 feet
Best season: March through July
Permits: none needed

Overview

A short hike leads to a powerful waterfall and introduces visitors to Hetch Hetchy. Cross O'Shaughnessy Dam and walk through the tunnel. Continue east along the shoreline over moderate climbs and drops. Early season visitors will first see Tueeulala Falls. Wapama Falls flows almost year-round. Mind your watch. Hetch Hetchy Road closes between 5:00 PM and 9:00 PM, depending on the season; check the National Park Service website or Hetch Hetchy Entrance Station.

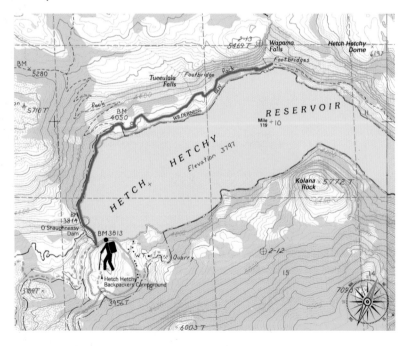

Elizabeth Lake

Distance: 4.8 miles round trip
Time: 2 to 3 hours
Difficulty: easy
Parking and trailhead: Tuolumne Meadows Campground, by the
restrooms on B loop, elevation 8,686 feet
Elizabeth Lake: elevation 9,487 feet
Best season: May through October
Permits: none needed for day use (no camping permitted)

Overview

Visit a tranquil glacier-carved lake in the shadow of Unicorn Peak. Enter
Tuolumne Meadows Campground and follow the signs to the trailhead.
Hike south through the forest. The first mile climbs most of the 800-foot
elevation gain. A use path that surrounds the lake is worth a lap and adds
about a mile. The ambitious can scramble onto 10,823-foot Unicorn Peak.
The return is all downhill.

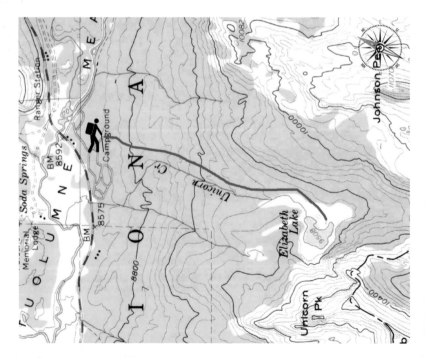

Lembert Dome

Distance: 2 miles
Time: 2 hours
Difficulty: easy to moderate
Parking and Trailhead: Dog Lake Trailhead, elevation 8,950 feet
Lembert Dome: elevation 9,450 feet
Best season: June through October
Permits: none needed

Overview

Take this fairly short and gentle hike to a novel perch atop a granite giant that commands an inspiring view of Tuolumne Meadows. Though the slanted traverse across granite may feel awkward, it requires no climbing expertise and many hikers make it each day in summer. The adventure can be extended to include a stop at Dog Lake.

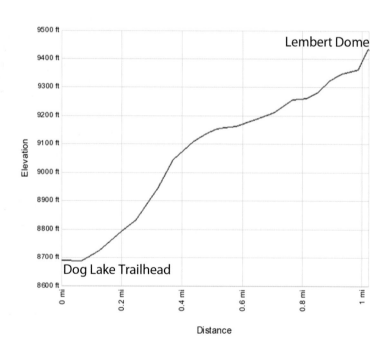

Hiking the hike

Hike northeast from Dog Lake parking area, cross Tioga Road and up the switchbacks beyond it. Turn left at the trail junction to begin your ascent on the east slope of Lembert Dome.

The view quickly becomes grand as hikers climb above the trees, but it's just a preview of the glory to come. Still ahead is the summit, which looks like a rounded knob. Hike west across the sloped granite toward its left side. To avoid its steep eastern face, aim slightly left to circle clockwise around the knob. Pass by the southern slope and instead ascend the gentler west face. Cathedral Peak, Mount Conness, Ragged Peak, and Mount Lyell are a few of the summits you can see on a clear day, plus the pristine Tuolumne River.

You could retrace your steps to return to the parking area, but if you've come this far already, consider visiting Dog Lake. Descend to the trail junction and turn left. Your path leads past the north face of Lembert Dome to a second junction. Turn right to climb slightly to the 9,170-foot lake, a great place to swim and eat lunch.

The shortest way back is to retrace your steps, but to loop around Lembert Dome adds only a half mile more. After leaving the lake, turn right at the trail junction to descend to Lembert Dome parking area. Cross Tioga Road and either take the trail or hike beside the highway to return to Dog Lake parking area. The entire journey including the summit, the lake, and the loop adds up to about 5 miles.

Insider tips

Hang on to your hat on the summit, it's windy up there!

Dog Lake's fishing alone makes it worth a visit.

Dog Lake

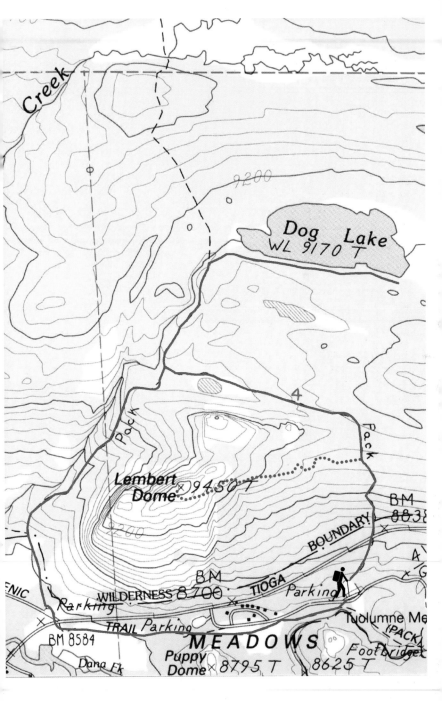

Bob Leang nears the summit of Lembert Dome.

Panorama Trail Loop

Distance: 10 miles
Time: 4 to 6 hours
Difficulty: moderate
Parking and trailhead: Glacier Point, elevation 7,213 feet
Best season: May through October
Permits: none needed for day use

Overview

Encompassing some of the park's most breathtaking scenery, the Panoramic Trail provides hikers with views of Illilouette Canyon, Liberty Cap, and Nevada Fall. Starting at Glacier Point, hikers also get to see the secretive Illilouette Fall. Complete this trek as a loop to add variety and to pass near Mount Starr King, or make it a point-to-point trek ending at Happy Isles.

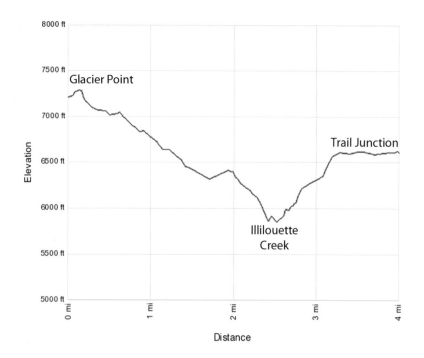

Illilouette Falls

Hiking the hike

Part of this loop covers the Panorama Trail which struts over the Merced River as it crashes down Nevada Fall and Vernal Fall. The second half explores a forest that burned decades ago and now provides a home for abundant young growth.

A large sign at Glacier Point shows the trailhead. Your first segment descends steadily as you hike south in Illilouette Ridge. At the first trail junction, turn left to drop more steeply into the canyon and to a view of 370-foot Illilouette Fall. In most parks, this would be a star attraction. In Yosemite, it ranks as a little-known gem. Illilouette Fall is only visible once from the trail, so stop to look. Then cross a bridge over Illilouette Creek and climb toward Panorama Cliff and its grand scenery.

By the next junction, hikers have gained an excellent vista of Nevada Fall and Liberty Cap. Now it's decision time. You could retrace your steps to Glacier Point, making the outing 8 miles long. You could descend northeast toward the John Muir and Mist trails and finish an 8.5-mile hike at Happy Isles; this is a great option if you prefer a point-to-point trek. But if you've already hiked the Muir and Mist trails, why not try something new? A right turn at the junction leads through a once-burned forest that's now full of young pines and wildflowers. Make a few more right turns to rejoin Illilouette Ridge. Then hike north to complete the loop and return to Glacier Point.

Insider tips

Keep an eye out for a trail veering left about a half mile after the bridge. An unsigned detour leads to Panorama Point and its awesome view of Half Dome. The vista has a steep drop and no guard rails. Be careful!

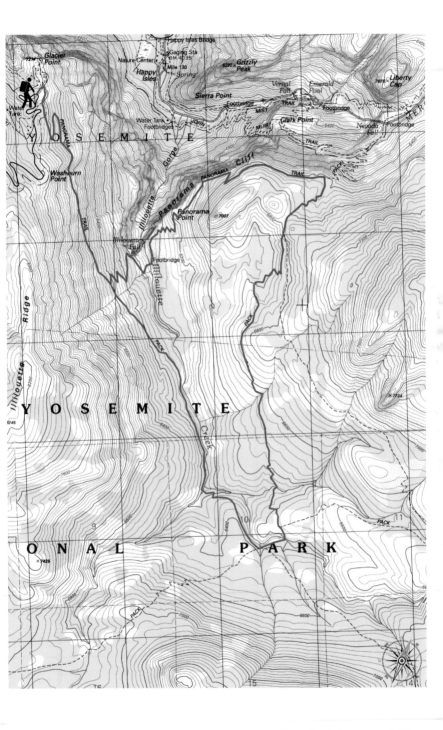

Chilnualna Falls

Distance: 7 miles round trip
Time: 3 to 5 hours
Difficulty: moderate
Parking and trailhead: dirt lot at the end of Chilnualna Falls Road, elevation 4,176 feet
Highest point: elevation 6,535 feet
Best season: March through June
Permits: none needed for day use

Overview

Chilnualna Falls consists of a 240-foot waterfall and several impressive cascades in a scenic and little-known part of Yosemite. The half-day outing near Wawona provides an interesting alternative to better-known day hikes in Yosemite Valley and Tuolumne Meadows. Elevation gain and considerable heat in summer months combine to keep many hikers away, but the undeterred discover a hidden jewel of the park.

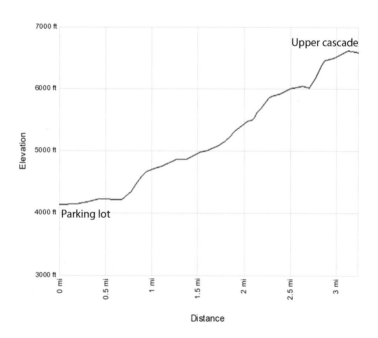

Hiking the hike

Many folks who've explored Yosemite for years have never even heard of this one, so first let's find it. From Wawona Road just north of Wawona, turn east on Chilnualna Falls Road. Drive about 1.5 miles past a school, grocery store, and cabins to a dirt parking area on the right.

A sign points to the trailhead and there's quickly a fork dividing hikers and horseback riders. Take the hikers' option, which passes by the picturesque Lower Cascade of Chilnualna Creek. After steep stone stairs, the trail turns and climbs as it leaves the creekside and winds its way northward up a ridge.

The climb eases as hikers ascend on switchbacks through a forest of oak, pine and cedar trees. Eventually you'll gain a view of the Wawona Dome and the surrounding forest basin. To the south stands the Mariposa Grove of Giant Sequoias.

Hikers will get their best view of Chilnualna Falls after turning east on the final switchback. Enjoy it here, for though it's a quarter-mile distant, the trail offers no closer view. But the worthy Upper Cascades of Chilnualna Creek await above the main waterfall. You've come this far, so go take a look before turning back.

Insider tips

Hike this one in the spring to beat the heat and catch the best waterfall viewing.

Stream crossings may be needed early in the season.

Distances and details

Start: Parking area
0.1 miles: Lower Cascades
3.3 miles: View of Chilnualna Falls
3.5 miles: Edge of Chilnualna Falls, Upper Cascades
7.0 miles: Return to parking area

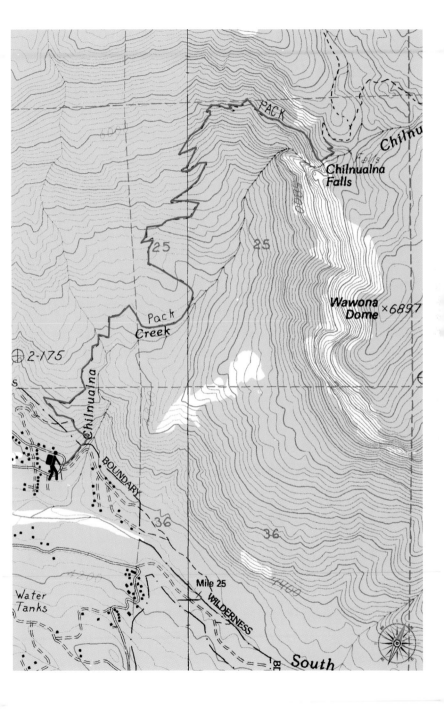

Vernal Fall and Nevada Fall Loop

Distance: 7.3 miles
Time: 2 to 4 hours
Difficulty: moderate
Parking: Curry Village or Yosemite Village day lot (take the free shuttle to Happy Isles)
Trailhead: Happy Isles, elevation 4,000 feet
Vernal Fall: elevation 5,070 feet
Nevada Fall: elevation 5,971 feet
Best season: March through November (some trail sections close in winter)
Permits: none needed for day use (no camping permitted)

Overview

Vernal Fall and Nevada Fall, twin scenic wonders, have enthralled millions of visitors on the park's most popular hike. Start on the Mist Trail, which literally puts hikers in touch with nature; prepare for a good soaking if you visit in spring. After climbing the stony steps beside Vernal Fall, your path leads on to Nevada Fall and back on the John Muir Trail.

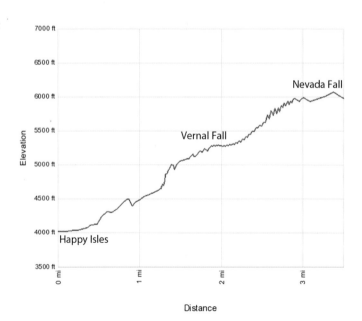

Vernal Fall

Hiking the hike

From Curry Village, walk a half mile or take the free bus to Happy Isles. Be sure to cross the bridge before turning right onto the Mist Trail. Here begins a steady 400-foot climb to Vernal Fall Bridge, where you'll get your first good look at the namesake 317-foot waterfall. This segment is a doable hike for most anyone, including families with small children.

Shortly after the bridge, hikers reach a fork in the trail. Some turn right up the switchbacks of the John Muir Trail, which rejoins the Mist Trail above Nevada Falls in about 3 miles. Most, though, turn left to stay on the Mist Trail, which ascends some 600 rocky stairs to the top of Vernal Fall. Now's the time to put on your rain gear. The drenching is a small price to pay for a great close-up look at the waterfall.

Enjoy the view from the top of Vernal Fall but please respect the warning signs and railing separating hikers from Emerald Pool. The algae-covered rock beneath the current is incredibly slick. Fatalities have occurred here when visitors waded just a short distance into the water, lost their footing and were swept over the fall.

For those who continue, the next attraction is Nevada Fall, about 2 miles away and 900 feet higher. The hiking remains rugged but less misty; rain gear won't be needed, unless it rains. Crowds thin out considerably by the top of Nevada Fall. Cross a footbridge just past Emerald Pool. About a mile later beneath Liberty Cap, turn right toward the Nevada Fall footbridge. Enjoy looking down on the raging Merced River and the 594-foot Nevada Fall waterfall.

Return the way you came or, for more variety and privacy, go back on the John Muir Trail. This affords hikers a terrific view of Nevada Fall and Liberty Cap, and another of Vernal Fall at Clark Point.

Insider tips

The only drinking fountain on the trip is found at Vernal Fall Bridge.

In winter and early spring, rangers close the Mist Trail segment between Vernal Fall Bridge and the top of Vernal Fall, as well as the John Muir Trail segment beneath Nevada Fall. Respect the closures for your safety and that of others.

The spray is not just drenching but freezing cold early in the year. Rain jackets, gloves and winter hats will come in handy.

This is also the start of the John Muir Trail; heavily-laden backpackers may be on their way to Mount Whitney, 211 miles away.

Distances and details

Start: Happy Isles
0.9 miles: Vernal Fall Bridge
1.0 miles: Junction of Mist Trail and John Muir Trail (stay left)
1.6 miles: Top of Vernal Fall (via Mist Trail)
3.5 miles: Top of Nevada Fall (via Mist Trail)
7.3 miles: Return to Happy Isles (via John Muir Trail)

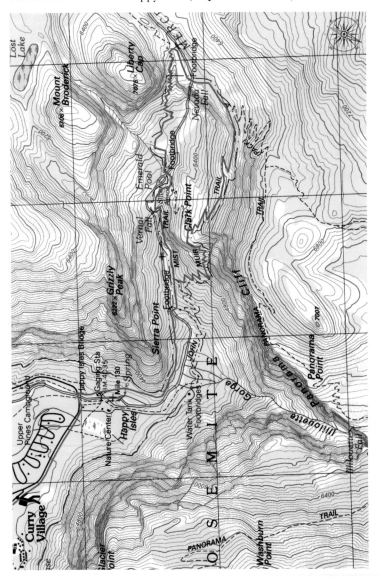

Four Mile Trail

Distance: 4.6 miles
Time: 4 to 6 hours
Difficulty: strenuous
Parking and trailhead: Four Mile Trailhead along Southside Drive, elevation 4,000 feet
Glacier Point: elevation 7,213 feet
Best season: May through October
Permits: none needed for day use

Overview

Four Mile Trail climbs from Yosemite Valley to Glacier Point, one of the finest vistas in the Sierra Nevada. The path gains about 3,200 feet in less than 5 miles, making for a physically demanding but worthwhile trek. You can make this an out-and-back trip of about 9 miles, though many hike up or down the trail and catch a ride to or from Glacier Point.

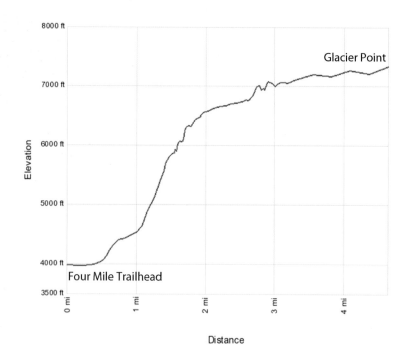

Sentinel Rock seen from Four Mile Trail

Hiking the hike

First you must decide: bottom to top, top to bottom, or both? Kudos to the ambitious few who hike out and back though most hikers seem to prefer a point-to-point outing. Delaware North, the park's concessionaire, runs several buses between Yosemite Valley and Glacier Point each day from late spring to early fall; visit yosemitepark.com for details. Following are instructions for hiking the uphill direction.

From Four Mile Trailhead, hike southeast as you look straight up to admire the grand Sentinel Rock. You will hike beneath and beside this proud granite tower for the next 3 miles. Early in the season, wildflowers will highlight your walk. Around a mile from the trailhead, you'll reach the most reliable stream crossing. Shortly after, begin the switchbacks that will lead you beside Sentinel and to fine vistas of the Cathedral Rocks, El Capitan, Yosemite Falls, and eventually Half Dome. About 3 miles up, you'll reach a short detour to Union Point. Take it; after your hard work, you deserve a rest at one of the best overviews of Yosemite Valley. More switchbacks follow through mostly wooded shade, flattening out in the last mile before you reach Glacier Point. Enjoy the magnificent view you have earned.

Insider tips

While hiking the downhill direction may sound appealing, consider that the steep drop will strain and pound your knees. Hiking uphill makes the view from Glacier Point your reward for a job well done.

Make sure to take enough water. There may be no running streams on the hike in a dry year or late in the season.

Half Dome and Tenaya Canyon

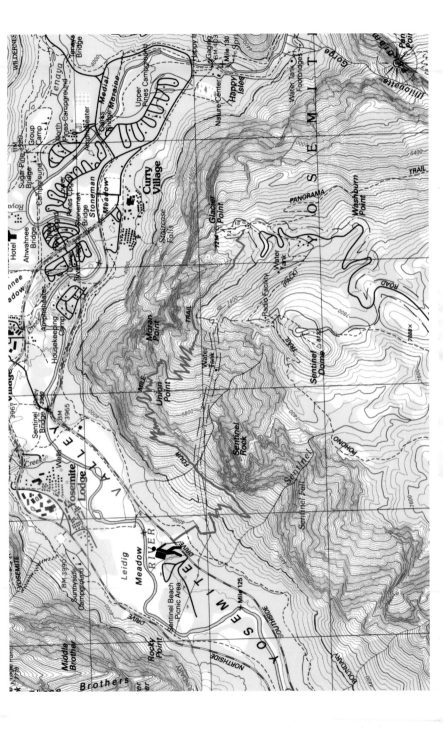

20 Yosemite Falls Trail

Distance: 6.8 miles round trip
Time: 5 to 7 hours
Difficulty: strenuous
Parking and trailhead: Camp 4, elevation 4,000 feet (park in the day use area)
Highest elevation: 6,692 feet
Yosemite Falls: elevation 6,579 feet
Best season: March through July; upper sections of the trail closed in winter
Permits: none needed for day use

Overview

Hikers on the Yosemite Falls Trail get up close and personal with the tallest waterfall in North America. Gaining 2,692 feet of elevation, the trail provides a challenging workout but rewards faithful travelers for every step. Those who go the distance get to stand beside the brink of a raging Upper Yosemite Fall.

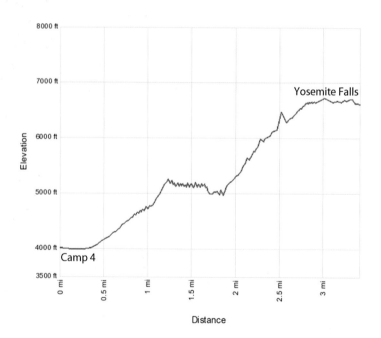

Hiking the hike

The trail begins north of Camp 4 and so does the climbing. Welcome to the world of switchbacks. You'll complete dozens of them and gain about 1,000 feet by Columbia Rock, a good spot to enjoy the view, rest, and assess your progress. This is the toughest part of the trail and does not offer a view of the waterfall, so if you're uncertain about whether to continue, consider that the best is yet to come.

From Columbia Rock, the route flattens for about a mile, still with some ups and downs; watch your step on the sandy switchbacks. Then you get your first look at Upper Yosemite Fall. Soon after that, a spur splits from the main trail to an outlook with the trip's best view of the entire 2,425-foot waterfall: Upper Yosemite Fall, the Middle Cascades, and Lower Yosemite Fall. The route's next landmark is the winter closure gate. Most reach this in about half the time they take to reach the trail's top.

Now the switchbacks return. Early in the season, a cool mist will ease your ascent. After the waterfall dries up in summer, expect a solar beating. There's manzanita and gravel requiring careful footing but no shade on the upper portion of the trail, which gains some 1,600 feet. Good thing you're tough!

The climbing ends at the upper winter gate. From here, a narrow and exposed path drops about a quarter-mile to a fenced viewing ledge beside the upper lip of the waterfall. Please stay away from the water, which has swept people over the falls to their deaths. However, those who stay on the path and behind the fence of the ledge can safely enjoy the majestic waterfall and awesome view of Yosemite Valley. Retrace your steps to return to Camp 4.

Insider tips

On the north side of the valley, this trail gets plenty of sun, making an early start beneficial and drinking enough water critical.

Yosemite Falls typically dries up in August, making the hike far less appealing in late summer and through the fall.

Hiking poles will be helpful on the trail's steep grade and many rocky sections.

Distances and details

Start: Camp 4
1.2 miles: Columbia Rock
3.4 miles: Top of Yosemite Falls
6.8 miles: Return to Camp 4

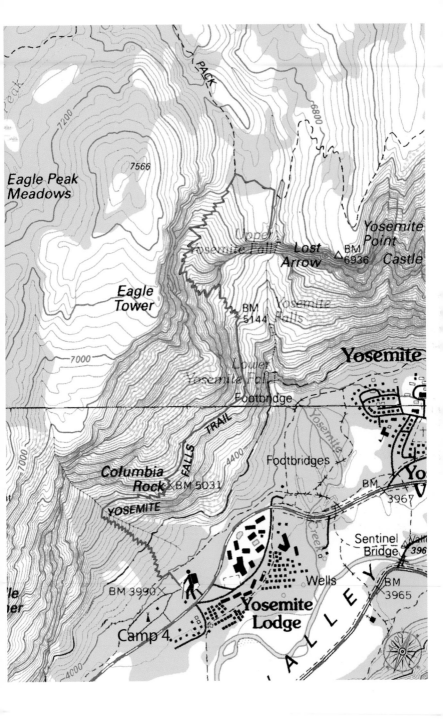

Eagle Peak
Meadows

7200

7566

Upper
Yosemite Falls

Lost
Arrow

Yosemite
Point

BM
6936

Castle

Eagle
Tower

BM
5144

Yosemite
Falls

7000

Lower
Yosemite Fall

Yosemite

Footbridge

Footbridges

Yosemite

Yosemite

FALLS TRAIL

4400

BM

Yo
V

7000

Columbia
Rock

XBM 5031

3967

YOSEMITE

Sentinel
Bridge

396

BM 3990 X

Wells

BM
3965

Camp 4

Yosemite
Lodge

VALLEY

4000

Tuolumne River in Glen Aulin

Backpacking

Introduction to Backpacking

Vast mountains, pristine lakes, and lush meadows await Yosemite backpackers, yet few people ever appreciate the park's backcountry offerings. While Yosemite Valley draws 95 percent of park visitors, the impressive and popular heart of Yosemite represents just 1 percent of the park's total area. More than 750 miles of wilderness trails invite hikers to explore Yosemite in a much different way than most tourists ever consider.

A few backcountry trips are suitable in spring but generally summer and fall are the best seasons for backpacking. Tioga Road and Glacier Point Road normally open in June. Temperatures are pleasant and mosquitoes disappear in the fall.

Consider elevation when planning a trip and give yourself time to acclimate in the high country.

Protect yourself from the sun with proper clothes and sunscreen. Your knees will thank you for using hiking poles on steep, rocky terrain. Stay on trails and do not take "short cuts."

Carry a map and compass on longer trips and do not rely exclusively on GPS devices.

Those venturing out overnight must protect their food from bears, and bears from their food. Bear cans are the best solution to this challenge. A well-packed can should hold enough food to last a backpacker for a week. Some popular backpacking camps like Glen Aulin have food storage lockers available. Hanging bags from trees is not recommended, nor legal; bears have become adept at accessing food stored this way. Please take care because bears suffer from becoming attracted to human food. Sometimes wildlife officials are even forced to kill bears that become aggressive.

Fires are permitted in existing fire rings only and not above 9,600 feet.

Backpackers are required to camp at least 100 feet from trails and water. Please bury human waste and pack out toilet paper and other trash.

Pets and bicycles are not permitted on trails.

Overnight travelers are required to obtain wilderness permits, either in person or through advance reservation. Backpackers without reservations may request permits at the park's wilderness centers starting at 11:00 AM one day prior to departure. There's no charge this way but also no guarantee of availability; permits run out at popular trailheads.

The park permits wilderness permit reservations up to 24 weeks in advance through fax, phone, or mail. See details at the nps.gov page for Yosemite wilderness permit reservations. The Yosemite Conservancy charges $5 for reservations plus $5 per person in the group.

Recommended gear:

boots
hiking poles
water bottles
map
compass
sunglasses (spares are also advised)
sunscreen (the stronger the better)
first aid kit
water filter and/or iodine tablets
sleeping bag
foam or inflatable mattress
tent or bivvy sack
stove with fuel
mess kit
matches and/or lighter
bear can
headlamp or flashlight
toilet paper
trowel
sandals

Optional items:

camera
GPS device
Mosquito netting and/or repellant

Author's journal of hiking the John Muir Trail, 1998:

I'd always wanted to see a wild bear up close, but when one finally appeared, Raffi, Joe, and I froze in shock. The giant casually wandered through Lyell Canyon like he owned the place, and if our furry friend was as hungry as he looked, our dinner would only be an appetizer. To scare him off, we started banging our pots and pans together. Not at all frightened, the bear eventually trudged away. But none of us ever forgot it and years later we still laugh about it. The Muir brings people close to nature, sometimes even closer than they would like. The trail also has a way of bringing old friends and new ones closer together.

Stars illuminate the Yosemite sky.
Photo by Dan Johanson

Cathedral Lakes

Distance: 7 miles round trip
Time: 2 days
Difficulty: easy to moderate
Parking and Trailhead: beside Tioga Road at Cathedral Lakes
Trailhead, elevation 8,585 feet
Best season: June through October
Permits: required for overnight travel; visit Tuolumne Meadows
Wilderness Center

Overview

This sojourn leads to some of the prettiest lakes in Yosemite. Hike south
through lodgepole pines on the John Muir Trail, climbing about 500 feet.
Then as Cathedral Peak comes into view, the hike flattens, passes through
meadows, and crosses Cathedral Creek. At the trail junction, turn right
for the lower lake or left for the upper one. Camping but no campfires are
permitted. This also makes a fine day trip.

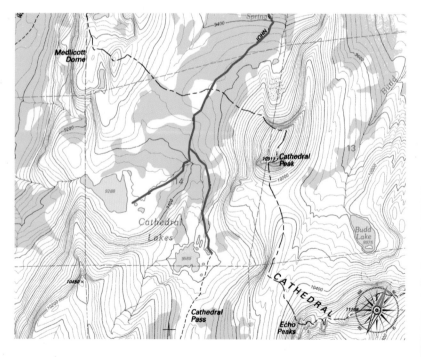

Young Lakes

Distance: 14 miles round trip
Time: 2 days
Difficulty: moderate
Parking: beside Tioga Pass Road near Lembert Dome (no overnight parking in Lembert Dome lot)
Trailhead: Lembert Dome, elevation 8,600 feet
Highest point: elevation 10,100 feet
Best season: June through September
Permits: required for overnight travel; visit Tuolumne Meadows Wilderness Center

Overview

By Yosemite standards, this overnight trip has a short hike and mild elevation changes. Those who take it reach a beautiful trio of lakes in the shadow of Ragged Peak. This trip is best as a loop, outbound on the Pacific Crest Trail and turning north toward Young Lakes, and returning on the more direct eastern trail passing Dog Lake.

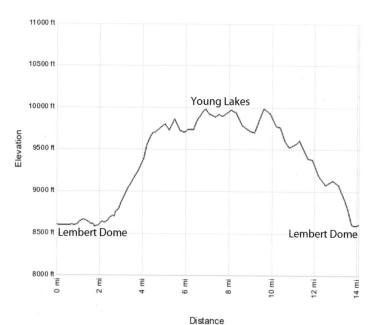

Hiking the hike

Start on the Pacific Crest Trail following the signs for Glen Aulin and quickly passing Soda Springs; stop and have some bubbly. After about 2 miles the trail for Young Lakes splits to the north and you will gradually climb through the forest and gain a grand vista of Tuolumne Meadows. A descent delivers you to the first and lowest of the lakes at 9,883 feet. If you choose to continue to the next lakes, between 100 and 300 feet higher in elevation, you can leave your pack at the first lake to hike unencumbered. Enjoy your night beneath nearby Ragged Peak, White Mountain, and Mount Conness.

To return, retrace your steps for 1.5 miles until the trail splits. The left (eastern) option saves about a mile and offers a unique view of Mount Lyell, Mount Ritter, and Banner Peak. Climbing and then descending, the route will eventually pass through a meadow and cross Delaney Creek. Another short climb and longer descent lead to a short turnoff to Dog Lake and then Lembert Dome before returning you to Tioga Road.

Insider tips

Most people visit just the lowest of the three Young Lakes, but trails lead to the other two.

Bring a rod and reel to enjoy fishing the lakes.

On the way back, take the short detour to visit Dog Lake.

Distances and details

Start: Lembert Dome
0.5 miles: Soda Springs
2.4 miles: Junction with trail to Young Lakes (go right)
7.6 miles: Young Lakes
9.1 miles: Junction with trail to Dog Lake (go left)
14 miles: Lembert Dome parking area

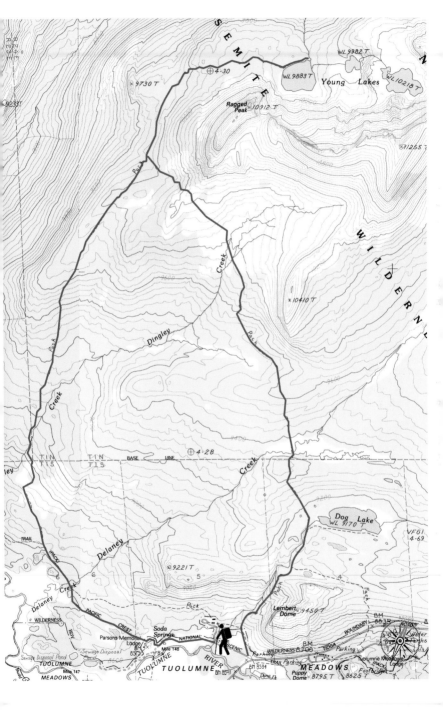

Tamarack Flat to El Capitan

Distance: 16.2 miles
Time: 2 days
Difficulty: moderate
Parking and trailhead: Tamarack Flat, elevation 6,300 feet
Highest point: elevation 7,735 feet
Best season: June and July
Permits: required for overnight travel; visit Yosemite Valley Wilderness Center

Overview

Compared to its rival Half Dome, El Capitan offers an easier hike, fewer permitting problems, and just as grand a view. Starting at Tamarack Flat, backpackers reach the summit by gaining about 1,450 feet. Returning to Tamarack Flat is one option, but the ambitious can tour past Eagle Peak and down the Yosemite Falls Trail to reach Yosemite Valley.

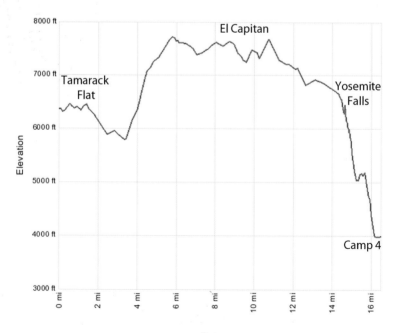

Hiking the hike

With El Capitan and Eagle Peak as highlight attractions, this journey deserves your attention. The trek is also shorter and easier than many popular Yosemite backpacking routes.

Time your visit wisely. Hikers must wait for the Tioga Road opening, usually in late spring. But the streams which supply water on the route dry up by late summer. June and July are ideal months.

Take Tioga Road east and, 3 miles from Crane Flat, turn right toward the Tamarack Flat Campground. Park here and start your hike on Old Big Oak Flat Road, heading east through a forest of lodgepole pines. Paved at first, the route steadily descends as you approach and cross a bridge over Cascade Creek. Good swimming holes are found here. Don't miss your left turn after the bridge where the trail parts from Old Big Oak Flat Road or you'll descend across talus into Yosemite Valley.

Next begins a climb through white firs and sugar pines to steep slopes covered with manzanita. Meadows full of wildflowers that await above will reward your toil. The best and only campsites are found beside Ribbon Creek, possibly the last source of water on the hike.

Take your time on the spur trail to fully enjoy the rounded summit of El Capitan. Here you have the same view as climbers who prepared for years to scale the great granite face.

If you continue to Yosemite Valley, your next attraction is just a few miles away. The summit of Eagle Peak, lauded by John Muir, is a worthy detour and a shame to miss if you're this close.

Then proceed east on the north rim to the Yosemite Falls Trail junction, turning right. Another short detour below will take you to the viewing ledge beside the upper brink of the roaring waterfall, an amazing sight (see map on page 95). The trail descends steeply for about 3 miles before delivering you to Camp 4, where you will surely find more El Cap climbers. Most likely, even they will not have experienced the journey you just completed.

Insider tips

When Ribbon Falls, west of El Capitan, is visible from Yosemite Valley, you'll know that Ribbon Creek is still flowing.

Though it borders Tamarack Creek, Tamarack Flat Campground has no treated water. Plan accordingly.

With the detour to Eagle Peak, the trip's mileage totals 17 miles.

Distances and details

Start: Tamarack Flat campground
2.2 miles: Trail junction (stay left)
2.3 miles: Cascade Creek
2.9 miles: Trail junction (stay left)
8.4 miles: El Capitan
10.8 miles: Eagle Peak
16.2 miles: Camp 4

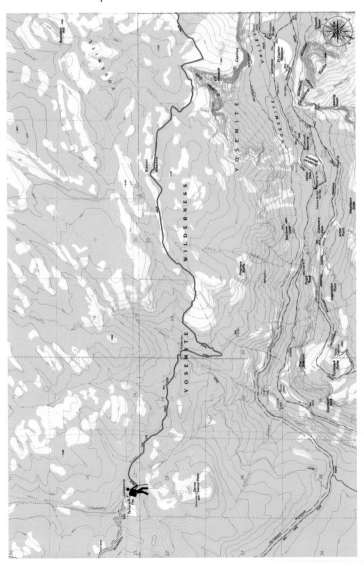

Ten Lakes Basin

Distance: 20.7 miles
Time: 2 to 4 days
Difficulty: moderate
Parking: beside Tioga Road near Tenaya Lake (no overnight parking in the picnic area beside Tenaya Lake)
Trailhead: Murphy Creek, elevation 8,153 feet
Highest point: elevation 9,929 feet
Best season: May through September
Permits: required for overnight travel; visit Tuolumne Meadows Wilderness Center

Overview

This outing combines glacier-carved granite domes and canyons, meandering streams, a lush forest, and a basin of serene lakes ideal for camping and fishing. Solitude will reign on the first half of this adventure as few hikers explore the Murphy Creek area. More enjoy the Ten Lakes Basin but there's plenty of privacy for those who get off the main trail and discover the smaller lakes.

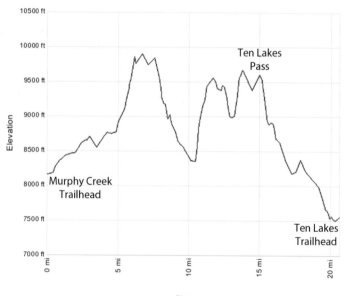

Hiking the hike

Your journey begins at Tenaya Lake and Polly Dome. Hike north beside Murphy Creek, gently climbing through lodgepole pines, which give way to granite slabs; watch for rock-pile trail markers.

Past the Polly Dome Lakes, turn left (west) toward Tuolumne Peak at the trail junction. The route winds counterclockwise around Tuolumne Peak leading to a river canyon heading north. Climb up switchbacks as the tree-ringed Ten Lakes replace the granite landscape. Choose from the many attractive campsites near the lakes.

When you're ready to leave the basin, climb west up to Ten Lakes Pass. Make sure to take a break and look back when you reach it to see the awesome Grand Canyon of the Tuolumne River and a panoramic view featuring Matterhorn Peak and Mount Conness. From the junction, a trail leads a mile south to the Grant Lakes. Turn right (west) to hike about 5 miles descending through the forest to the Ten Lakes Trailhead.

Insider tips

The Ten Lakes area is popular with backpackers, but approaching from Murphy Creek may help you get a wilderness permit more easily and makes a point-to-point rather than an out-and-back outing.

Many hikers can complete this trek in two days, but take three to enjoy this little-known Yosemite treasure.

Fishing is best in the lower lakes.

Distances and details

Start: Murphy Creek Trailhead
3.1 miles: Trail junction (go left)
3.5 miles: Trail junction (go right)
13 miles: First of the Ten Lakes
16.7 miles: Ten Lakes Pass
20.7 miles: Ten Lakes Trailhead

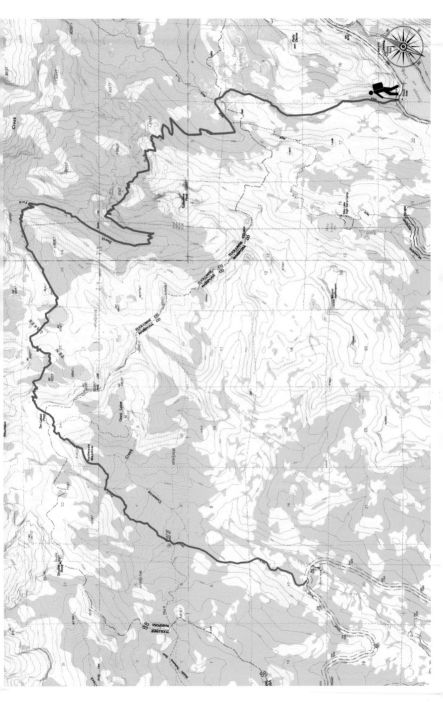

Grand Canyon of the Tuolumne River

Distance: 29 miles
Time: 3 days
Difficulty: moderate to strenuous
Parking: beside Tioga Pass Road near Lembert Dome (no overnight parking in Lembert Dome lot)
Trailhead: Lembert Dome, elevation 8,600 feet
Lowest point: elevation 4,257 feet
Best season: June to September
Permits: required for overnight travel; visit Tuolumne Meadows Wilderness Center

Overview

Experience the Tuolumne River by hiking through the canyon it carved. This trek features water in a multitude of forms: dramatic waterfalls, rushing cascades, worthy fishing, fun swimming holes, the pleasant sound of a roaring river, lots of beautiful water-sculpted granite, and even a natural water slide. The Tuolumne ultimately provides water for millions, yet only a few enjoy the river in the pristine wilderness.

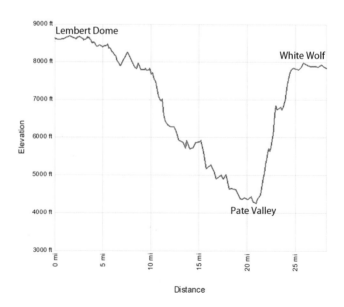

Hiking the hike

This point-to-point hike is equally enjoyable westbound or eastbound. Either way, it starts downhill and finishes uphill. These directions lead from east to west, which requires less overall climbing and which most backpackers prefer.

Park beside the highway near Lembert Dome, or beside the dirt road leading toward a stable (in the main lot beside Lembert Dome, no overnight parking is permitted). Your hike follows the dirt road to a gate and continues past it toward Parsons Memorial Lodge, built by the Sierra Club in 1915. Soon your route approaches and then parallels the Tuolumne River. After a climb, the trail descends into a wooded area. Shortly after crossing a footbridge, you'll see Tuolumne Falls and later White Cascade. Descend toward a bridge over the Tuolumne. Across is the popular Glen Aulin High Sierra Camp. You could spend your first night here, but consider continuing downriver another mile or so where a pleasant meadow offers more privacy.

The next segment is the highlight of the trip, starting with three wonders in a row. As the trail descends into the river canyon, hikers pass California Falls, Le Conte Falls, and Waterwheel Falls in less than 2 miles.

Tuolumne Falls

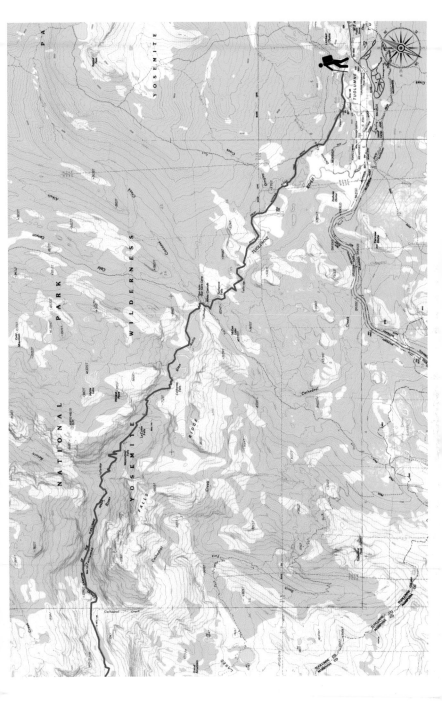

You'll drop elevation all day, more than 3,000 feet if you hike to the canyon's bottom, and on the way you'll enjoy every foot of the rushing river as it plunges beside granite peaks and through boulders, meadows, and trees.

Don't miss the best swimming hole of the area, found about 3 miles east of Pate Valley. If you can handle a long hike from Glen Aulin, camp your second night in lush Pate Valley, full of pines, oaks, redwoods, ferns, and maples (watch out for poison oak, though).

By the third day, your pack will be lighter, which will help your climb of nearly 4,000 feet out of the river canyon. From Pate Valley, the trail traces the Tuolumne for about another mile before beginning a long climb up the southern canyonside. Your efforts will pay off with a fine view of Hetch Hetchy as you ascend. Before the trail leaves the canyon, a split provides a choice for the final miles. Turn left to take the shortest and steepest path to White Wolf, or turn right to hike a little longer and visit Harden Lake on the way. If you want to treat yourself at the White Wolf Lodge, no one can say you didn't earn it.

Insider tips

This hike involves many stream crossings, especially early in the season. If you bring a pair of sandals, you won't have to soak your boots to ford them.

A heavy snow year means a heavy mosquito season. If the waterfalls are big, come prepared!

Distances and details

Start: Lembert Dome
0.5 miles: Soda Springs
4.8 miles: Tuolumne Falls
5.5 miles: Glen Aulin High Sierra Camp
6.9 miles: California Falls
8.0 miles: LeConte Falls
8.2 miles: Waterwheel Falls
19.2 miles: Pate Valley
29 miles: White Wolf

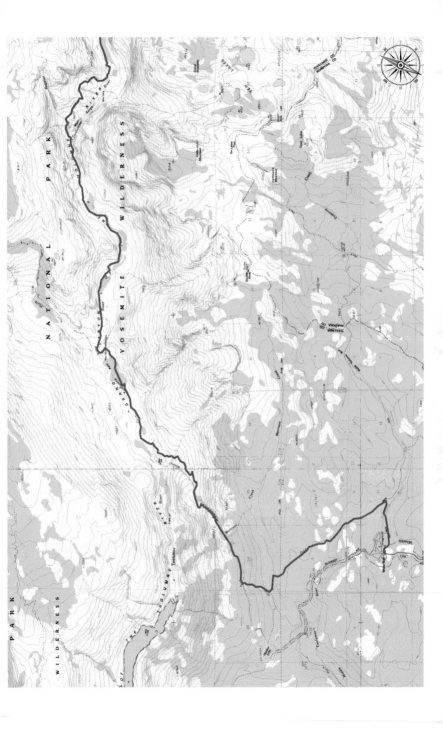

Hetch Hetchy and Vernon Lake Loop

Distance: 23 miles
Time: 2 to 3 days
Difficulty: moderate
Parking: lot beside O'Shaughnessy Dam at Hetch Hetchy Reservoir
Trailhead: O'Shaughnessy Dam, 3,820 feet
Highest point: elevation 7,637 feet
Best season: March through October
Permits: required for overnight travel; visit Hetch Hetchy Entrance Station

Overview

Get to know the valley John Muir and environmentalists fought to preserve. Though dammed, Hetch Hetchy still has great scenic beauty and a fraction of the visitation in other parts of Yosemite. This hike passes three waterfalls and explores Hetch Hetchy Valley, the reservoir, its watershed, and Lake Vernon. With lower elevation than many other backcountry trips, the loop appeals to backpackers for most of the year.

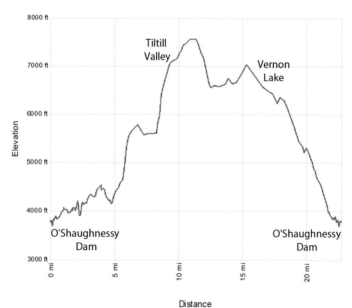

Kolana Rock and Hetch Hetchy Reservoir

Hiking the hike

Say, isn't that El Capitan, Yosemite Falls, and Sentinel Rock? Nope, it's Hetch Hetchy Dome, Wapama Falls, and Kolana Rock. Hetch Hetchy Valley's resemblance to its more popular neighbor is nothing less than surreal. This trip will help you see for yourself and explore some pristine backcountry as a bonus.

Backpackers can enjoy this loop in either direction but may want to proceed counterclockwise in spring. That's because Wapama Falls sometimes overflows the footbridge beneath it. By hiking along the reservoir first, backpackers can ensure the bridge is passable before committing to the loop. This is only an issue at peak flow after a heavy winter.

Walk across O'Shaughnessy Dam and through the tunnel. Continue east along the shoreline over moderate climbs and drops, passing Tueeulala Falls and Wapama Falls. Later, you'll reach Rancheria Falls. The campground here is a good place to spend a night, but store food properly because bears like it too.

The next leg climbs to the lush Tiltill Valley, crossing Tiltill Creek. Then the trail climbs over the flank of Mount Gibson on the way to Lake Vernon, a little-known gem and another good overnight spot. The lake's outlet forms Falls Creek, which flows down a chute of granite on its way to Wapama Falls.

From the lake, hike southwest over some modest ups and downs. At Beehive Meadow, there's a spring and a trail junction; stay left. You'll pass through an area of burned forest and pass a small pond between the next junction; stay left again. Descend on switchbacks over old Lake Eleanor Road. This segment will provide the best views (and pictures) of Hetch Hetchy Reservoir and Kolana Rock. At the bottom, turn right to return through the tunnel and across the dam.

Insider tips

Watch out! Due to its low elevation, this is one of the few Yosemite hikes with poison oak.

Hetch Hetchy Road closes between 5:00 PM and 9:00 PM, depending on the season; check the National Park Service website or the Hetch Hetchy Entrance Station.

Hetch Hetchy has a backpackers campground where wilderness permit holders can spend one night before and one night after their trips for $5 per person.

Distances and details

Start: O'Shaughnessy Dam
1.5 miles: Tueeulala Falls
2.5 miles: Wapama Falls
6.3 miles: Rancheria Falls
9 miles: Tiltill Valley
15.8 miles: Vernon Lake
19.1 miles: Beehive Meadow
23 miles: Return to O'Shaughnessy Dam

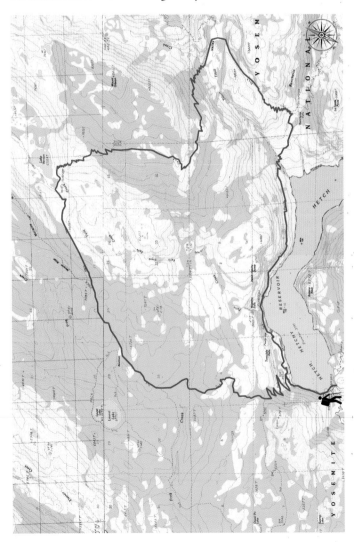

Lake Vernon reflects neighboring peaks in morning light.

John Muir Trail: Happy Isles to Tuolumne Meadows

Distance: 23 miles
Time: 2 to 4 days
Difficulty: moderate to strenuous
Parking: trailhead parking area (southwest of road between Curry Village and Happy Isles)
Trailhead: Happy Isles, elevation 4,000 feet
Highest point: elevation 9,929 feet
Best season: June through October
Permits: required for overnight travel; visit Yosemite Valley Wilderness Center

Overview

This first segment of the John Muir Trail leads above Vernal and Nevada waterfalls, through Little Yosemite Valley and past the Cathedral Lakes. While the route gains about 6,000 feet, it stays close to water and features exquisite scenery. If you've ever dreamed of hiking the John Muir Trail, try this portion as a trial run. You may feel compelled to complete the 218-mile journey.

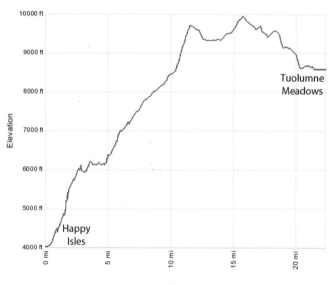

Liberty Cap and Nevada Fall

Hiking the hike

After parking at the trailhead area, walk or take the shuttle to Happy Isles. Cross the bridge before turning right onto the John Muir Trail (here it overlaps with the Mist Trail). Begin a steady 400-foot climb to Vernal Fall Bridge, where you'll get your first good look at the namesake 317-foot waterfall.

Shortly after the bridge, hikers reach a fork in the trail. Turn right to stay on the John Muir Trail, which will climb up switchbacks above the Mist Trail and Vernal Fall; stop at Clark Point for a great photo. Hike toward and past Nevada Fall, crossing the footbridge over the Merced River. If you haven't taken a break yet, stop here and enjoy the ambiance, but do not attempt to swim above the waterfall.

Red Peak. Photo by Dan Johanson

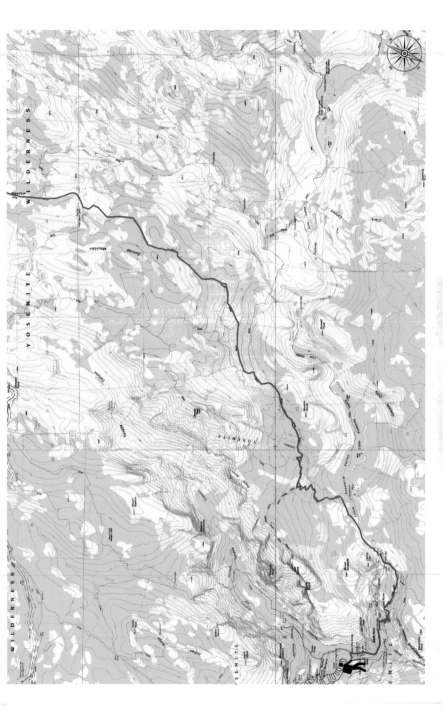

Continue east up the river canyon as you pass beneath stately Liberty Cap and into Little Yosemite Valley. Soon you will reach a trail junction where the John Muir Trail continues to the left. But most will want to go right about a half mile to the Little Yosemite Valley backpackers campground. This is the first legal camping area Muir hikers reach. There's no charge or check-in; just pick an open site and pitch your tent.

Backtrack to reconnect with the Muir; there's actually a northbound connector trail that permits a little short cut. Now it's time to climb the switchbacks that lead to Half Dome. Soon hikers reach a trail junction where the Muir and Half Dome trails split ways. You need a permit if you want to climb the popular granite giant (see page 184). If you have one, enjoy the adventure! If not, turn right to stay on the Muir. A half mile later, a side trail leads to Clouds Rest, an outstanding summit that requires no permit, though a detour from here will take much of the day.

The Muir follows Sunrise Creek through a valley before climbing to Sunrise High Sierra Camp. From here, a side trail leads to the Sunrise Lakes about 2 miles distant, where you'll find private and secluded campsites. Winding up Long Meadow, the Muir passes the needle-like Columbia Finger; on its west side, a class 3 scramble leads to the summit. Backpackers reach the high point of this segment as they traverse Tressider Peak; be sure to stop and look back at the fine view of southern Yosemite.

Following Cathedral Pass, you will descend to the pristine Cathedral Lakes. The Muir passes right by the upper lake. The lower lake requires a half-mile detour (see page 102). Both are magnificent and worthy of your time.

On the final miles from here to Tuolumne Meadows, you will likely meet day hikers and rock climbers as you drop about a thousand feet and begin to transition out of the wilderness. Backpackers can exit at the Cathedral Lakes Trailhead, though the Muir actually turns east just short of the Tioga Road and leads past the visitor center to the campground. This may be a more pleasant route to Tuolumne's store and grill, where you should treat yourself to a meal and contemplate the remaining 193 miles of the John Muir Trail.

Merced River in Little Yosemite Valley

Insider tips

While proper food storage is required everywhere in Yosemite, be especially careful in Little Yosemite Valley. This is the most popular spot in the Yosemite wilderness, for bears as well as people!

If you can't score a permit to depart from Happy Isles, try hiking from Glacier Point on the Panorama Trail to Little Yosemite Valley. That permit can be easier to get, and for those who've already hiked around Vernal Falls and Nevada Falls, the less-crowded variation features new scenery and gets you to the same final destination.

Distances and details

Start: Happy Isles
0.9 miles: Vernal Fall Bridge
1.0 miles: Junction of Mist Trail and John Muir Trail
2.0 miles: Clark Point
3.8 miles: Nevada Falls
4.4 miles: Junction with trail to Little Yosemite Valley campground
5.9 miles: Junction with trail to Half Dome (go right)
13.7 miles: Sunrise High Sierra Camp
17.3 miles: Cathedral Pass
18.4 miles: Junction with trail to Lower Cathedral Lake (stay right)
23 miles: Tuolumne Meadows store

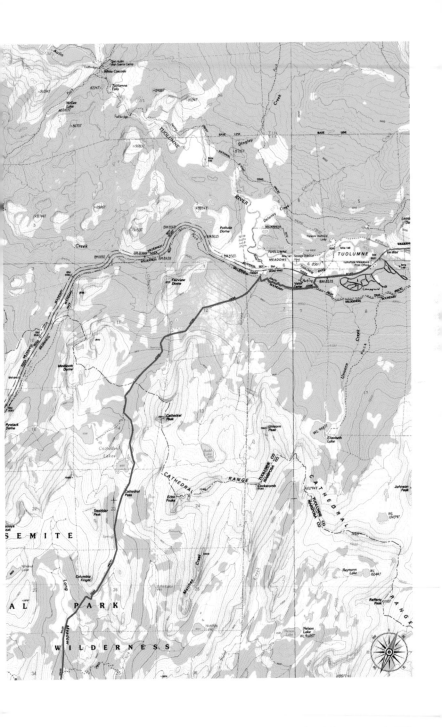

28

John Muir Trail: Tuolumne Meadows to Devils Postpile

Distance: 28.8 miles
Time: 3 to 4 days
Difficulty: strenuous
Parking and trailhead: Tuolumne Meadows Wilderness Center, elevation 8,680 feet
Donohue Pass: elevation 11,056 feet
Best season: June through October
Permits: required for overnight travel; visit Tuolumne Meadows Wilderness Center

Overview

This is the most accessible and among the prettiest segments of the John Muir Trail. Less crowded than the Muir's beginning at Happy Isles, the Tuolumne Meadows to Devils Postpile section generally has better availability of wilderness permits. Starting at a high trailhead, the route climbs over Donohue Pass and then quickly plunges into a scenic wonderland of dramatic peaks and pristine lakes.

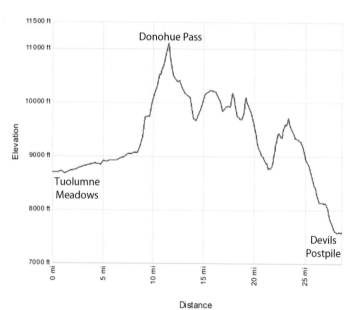

Tuolumne River

Hiking the hike

At the Tuolumne Meadows Wilderness Center, pick up the John Muir Trail heading east through a meadow and past the rangers' office. Follow the signs for Donohue Pass and cross a bridge over the Lyell Fork of the Tuolumne River. Hike south beside the river for several miles, past prominent Potter Point, and to the end of Lyell Canyon. This is a good area to camp the first night.

Next begins a long climb toward Donohue Pass. The trail ascends many switchbacks and crosses over a bridge before a sharp turn to the east leads to a final ascent. At the pass, backpackers leave Yosemite and enter the Ansel Adams Wilderness. Descend into a picturesque basin where Rush Creek meanders through a grassy meadow and granite boulders. There are some worthy campsites here. Hikers in early season will need to ford the creek near the junction with the Marie Lakes Trail. Several other fords await over the remaining miles to Devils Postpile.

More switchbacks lead down to the Rush Creek Forks before a short climb up to Island Pass. Now you're looking right at three spectacular sights: Mount Ritter, Banner Peak, and Thousand Island Lake. Descend to the east toward the blue water filled with rocky islets. Camping is prohibited

Lyell Canyon

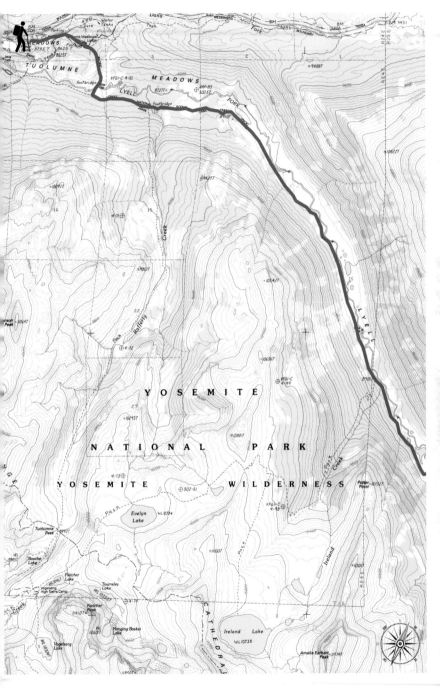

within a quarter-mile of the lake outlet, though there are plenty of other appealing areas. Stop for pictures here, at least. It's a breathtaking place.

From here on the trail meets many junctions. Simply follow the well-marked Muir as it passes Ruby Lake, Garnett Lake, Shadow Lake, Rosalie Lake, Gladys Lake, and others; there's plenty of worthy fishing here for motivated anglers. Many of these areas have camping restrictions. Please comply with the signs to protect this popular and well-used area. From here on, expect to encounter many hikers and campers approaching from the Mammoth Lakes area.

A long descent of a volcanic ridge through lodgepole pines precedes your arrival at Devils Postpile, through which the Muir continues south toward Mount Whitney. To exit here, look for an intersection with the Pacific Crest Trail shortly after entering the national monument. Take the southeast route of the four-way junction leading to a bridge across the Middle Fork of the San Joaquin River about a half mile away. After crossing the bridge, backpackers arrive at a T-junction. If you've never seen the Devils Postpile, make the short detour to the right to examine the fascinating basalt columns that inspired the park's name. Take the left turn to reach the parking area, regrettably return to civilization and begin planning your next adventure.

Mount Ritter and Banner Peak

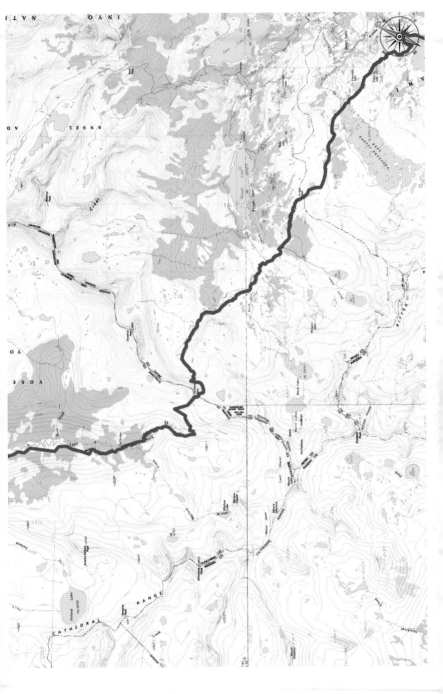

Insider tips

Hiking over Donohue Pass with a backpack will test your fitness and acclimation. Spending a few nights at altitude first will help.

Bears abound along this route so be especially careful with food storage.

Transportation on this point-to-point trek will require some car shuttling or a helpful driver. Be advised that the narrow, windy road from Mammoth Lakes to Devils Postpile is closed to incoming private traffic (but permits outbound traffic) from June through September between 7:30 AM and 5:30 PM, when a shuttle service operates.

Distances and details

Start: Tuolumne Meadows Wilderness Center
13.8 miles: Donohue Pass
20.9 miles: Thousand Island Lake
26.4 miles: Shadow Lake
28.0 miles: Trail Junction (go straight)
28.5 miles: Bridge across San Joaquin River
28.8 miles: Devils Postpile parking area

Devils Postpile

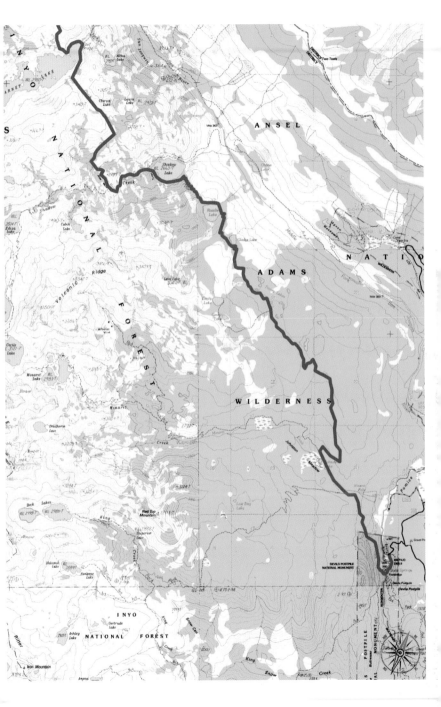

Pacific Crest Trail: Tuolumne Meadows to Sonora Pass

Distance: 75 miles
Time: 6 to 8 days
Difficulty: very strenuous
Parking: beside Tioga Pass Road near Lembert Dome (no overnight parking in Lembert Dome lot)
Trailhead: Lembert Dome, elevation 8,600 feet
Highest point: elevation 10,759 feet
Best season: June to September
Permits: required for overnight travel; visit Tuolumne Meadows Wilderness Center

Overview

This rugged section of the Pacific Crest Trail climbs, drops, climbs more, drops more, climbs even more, and drops even more from Yosemite to the Emigrant Wilderness. It's a physically demanding, high-elevation hike and not for beginners. But for those ready for it, the trek delivers solitude and access to rarely-seen peaks and seldom-visited lakes.

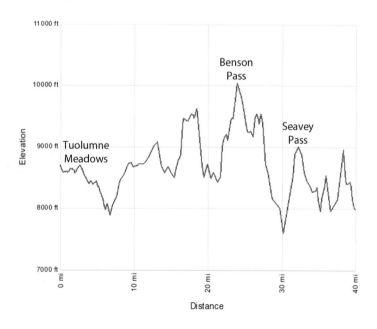

Smedberg Lake and Volunteer Peak

Hiking the hike

Backpackers can travel this point-to-point trek hiking either north or south. This guide recommends hiking north from Tuolumne Meadows to start at lower elevation and on less-demanding terrain. Those who begin at Sonora Pass not only start their hike at 9,623 feet but must immediately climb to the hike's highest point at 10,759 feet with full packs, many of the hikers coming from sea level with no altitude acclimation! Instead, start in Yosemite, where the trailhead is a thousand feet lower, and break into the hike with a few fairly mild days.

Before leaving, though, give a thought to transportation. If you drive to Yosemite, how do you get back to your vehicle from Sonora Pass? Or if you leave a car at Sonora Pass, how do you get to Yosemite? Public transportation offers no solution to this problem. Most hikers shuttle vehicles with the help of friends or family.

Park beside the highway near Lembert Dome, or beside the dirt road leading toward the stables (in the Lembert Dome lot, no overnight parking is permitted). Your hike follows the dirt road to a gate and continues past it toward Soda Springs. Pause here to try the naturally carbonated water bubbling from the ground. Soon your route approaches and then parallels the Tuolumne River. After a climb, the trail descends into a wooded area. Shortly after crossing a footbridge, you'll see Tuolumne Falls and later White Cascade. Descend toward a bridge over the Tuolumne. Across is the popular Glen Aulin High Sierra Camp, where most passersby stay a night.

Continue north into Cold Canyon. The trail will climb steadily until dropping into Virginia Canyon. There are worthy campsites along McCabe Creek and Return Creek. But if you can, climb the switchbacks out of the canyon and push on another 3 miles to Miller Lake. This will position you to reach coveted Benson Lake on the next day.

From Miller Lake, descend into Matterhorn Canyon and cross its creek as the trail turns southwest. Then climb out of the canyon and over Benson Pass on your way to Smedberg Lake. This is a great place to stop for lunch, swim, and fish.

The next segment passes a spur trail to Benson Lake. Though it's a detour from the Pacific Crest Trail, you really shouldn't miss it (see page 156).

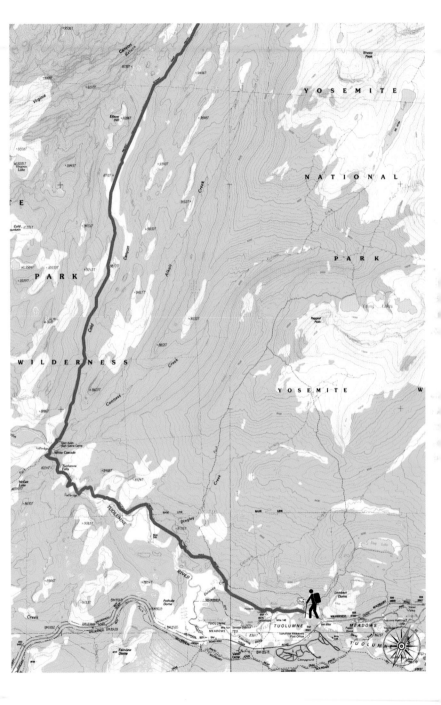

From the Benson Lake detour to Seavey Pass, hikers gain 1,600 feet in less than 3 miles. Take your time and enjoy the ponds and small lakes along the way. Then your path descends and turns west into Kerrick Canyon. About 3 miles down canyon, turn north and cross the creek, which can be challenging in the early season. Now begins the next climb and descent into Stubblefield Canyon. After that, take a break and decide if you're up for another few miles and few thousand feet of up and down. If not, camp here near the creek. If you can make another push, though, climb over Macomb Ridge and push on toward Wilma Lake. A shady and pleasant walk leads to this lake where a ranger cabin stands.

Turning north, the Pacific Crest Trail leads past Chittenden, Kendrick, Keyes, and Bigelow peaks while passing through Grace Meadow, climbing gradually toward Dorothy Lake. After the steeper climbs you accomplished earlier, this one will feel pleasantly mild. Dorothy Lake offers tree-sheltered campsites and you don't have to be an expert to catch a fish here.

After climbing to Dorothy Lake Pass, hikers depart Yosemite and enter the Toiyabe National Forest. Passing Stella and Bonnie lakes, descend to Lake Harriet and continue north. Just past two ponds is a junction; turn

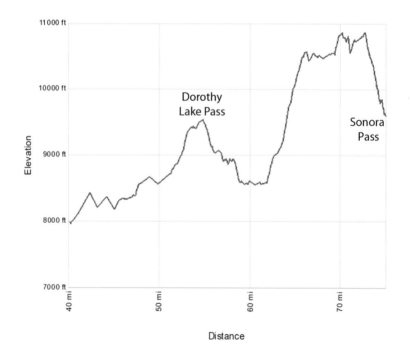

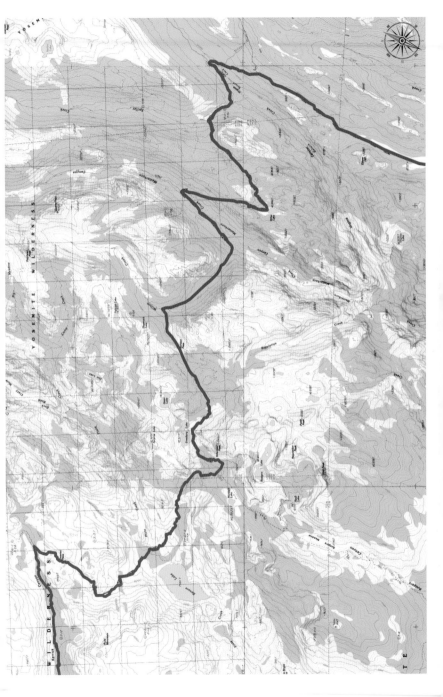

northwest to stay on the Pacific Crest Trail and head toward the West Fork West Walker River. You will pass Lower Long Lake on your way to Walker Meadows. Now you're close to civilization again and may start to see some day hikers.

Soon your path turns west through rocky Kennedy Canyon. Even early in the day, consider camping here because few appealing options and precious little water are found between here and Sonora Pass. But hikers making an early start after spending a night here can reach their trek's end in a day. Make sure to fill water bottles before leaving.

Start by climbing westward to the saddle above Kennedy Canyon. Then your path turns north and becomes a jeep road that zig-zags up

Peaks overlooking Dorothy Lake

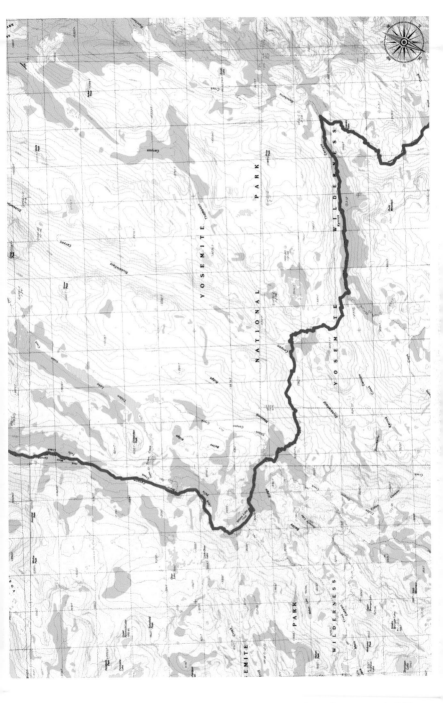

long switchbacks to a high ridge well above the tree line. After gaining the ridge, the jeep road drops down to Leavitt Lake but the Pacific Crest Trail turns northwest and traverses a volcanic ridge. You're now in the Emigrant Wilderness of the Stanislaus National Forest. Eventually snow and snowmelt may give you a chance to refill your water bottles. When the trail passes beneath Leavitt Peak, you have the option to scramble up its rocky slopes to a 11,569-foot summit. The 800-foot climb is a worthy detour on the right day.

Continuing north past Latopie Lake, be wary of steep and possibly icy snowfields, especially early in the day and season, between here and the road. Your final miles twist and turn as you descend more than a thousand feet past whitebark pines and seasonal wildflowers before reaching Sonora Pass.

Emigrant Wilderness near Sonora Pass

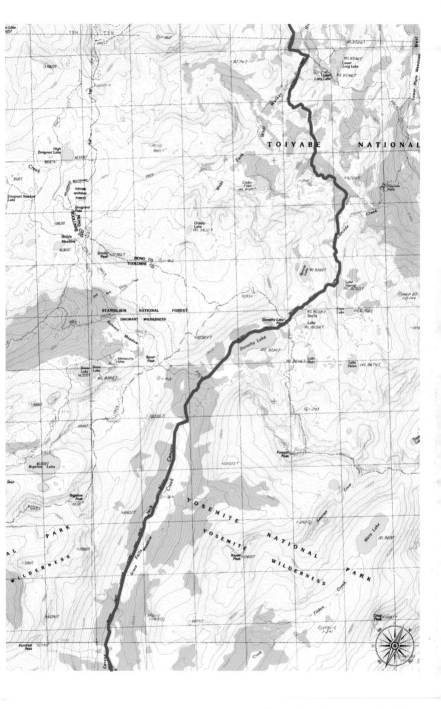

Insider tips

Take a fishing license and pole. There are many good fishing opportunities and fresh trout will taste better than freeze-dried backpacking fare after a few days.

Consider carrying crampons and ice axes in the early season to safely cross snowfields in the Emigrant Wilderness.

Distances and details

Start: Lembert Dome
0.5 miles: Soda Springs
4.8 miles: Tuolumne Falls
5.5 miles: Glen Aulin High Sierra Camp
17 miles: Miller Lake
23.8 miles: Benson Pass
25.7 miles: Smedberg Lake
29.9 miles: Junction with trail to Benson Lake
32.6 miles: Seavey Pass
44.4 miles: Wilma Lake
53.9 miles: Dorothy Lake
54.9 miles: Dorothy Lake Pass
60.4 miles: West Fork West Walker River bridge
63.9 miles: Kennedy Canyon
67 miles: Junction with trail to Leavitt Lake (turn left)
75 miles: Sonora Pass

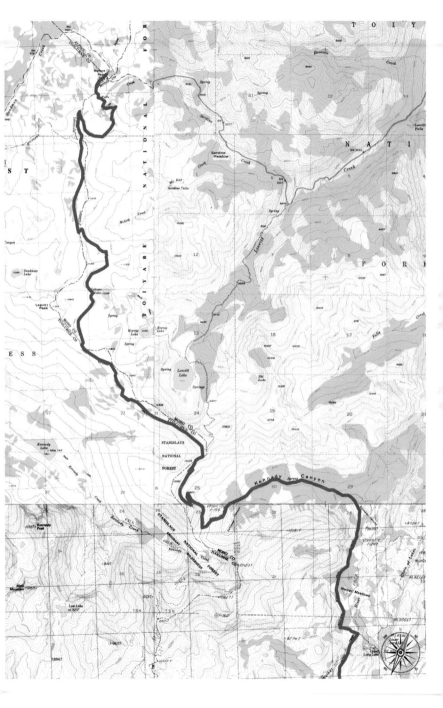

Pacific Crest Trail Side Trip: Benson Lake

Distance: 0.8 miles round trip
Time: 1 hour of hiking (but plan some leisure time here)
Difficulty: easy
Starting point: Pacific Crest Trail between Smedberg Lake and Seavey Pass, elevation 7,585 feet
Benson Lake: elevation 7,581 feet
Best season: June to October
Permits: required for overnight travel; visit Tuolumne Meadows Wilderness Center

Overview

If you're hiking through Yosemite's northern backcountry, you have to visit this beautiful beach. Take the spur trail off the Pacific Crest Trail through the damp and shady forest to the lake's northeast shore near the Piute Creek inlet. Enjoy the white sand, perfectly blue water, fishing and solitude of the "Benson Riviera." Try to arrange your hike to spend a night here.

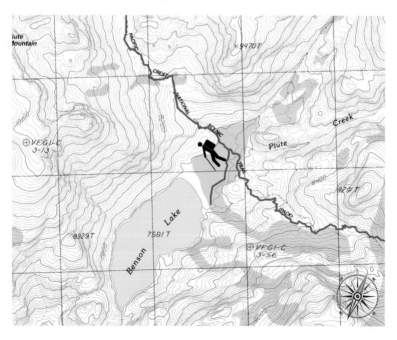

A climber exalts atop Half Dome.

Mountain Climbing

Introduction to Mountain Climbing

Scores of mountain peaks beckon in Yosemite, many of them attainable with minimal gear and expertise. Quite a few summits can be reached in one day by the reasonably fit. Those who climb them earn a bird's eye view of the park and a terrific sense of accomplishment.

The routes in this book require no specialized gear unless noted. Hiking at high elevation is a serious undertaking, though, and many people will require some time to acclimate before challenging themselves on alpine peaks. Drinking plenty of water will help.

The described mountains each have established routes to their summits. "Established" is a relative term, however, and staying on route is easier on some peaks than on others. Mind your surroundings and your progress using a map and compass and do not rely exclusively on GPS devices.

None of the suggested trips should require rope or other rock climbing gear, but there will be steep terrain and possibly snow and ice early in the season.

Summer and fall offer the best climbing conditions, as these summits will be snowbound in winter and spring.

Yosemite sees its share of afternoon thunderstorms. For that reason, start early if you're heading up a mountain and turn around if you see dark gray clouds rolling in.

Pets and bicycles are not permitted on trails. Please pack out all trash.

Permits are not required for day trips, with the exception of hikers summiting Half Dome; wilderness permits are required for overnight backcountry travel.

This guide uses standard mountaineering terminology to describe the difficulty of terrain:

Class 1: easy walking

Class 2: simple scrambling on hilly or rough territory

Class 3: scrambling on steep ground using handholds and footholds

Class 4: simple climbing on steeper and harder terrain with dangerous fall potential

Class 5: climbing requiring gear, ropes, and belays for protection

The rating indicated in each chapter indicates the most difficult terrain on the described route, though much of the route will be easier and often class 1. If the terrain seems more difficult than the rating would suggest, that's often an indication that the climber is off route!

This leads to a final point, listed last but not least important: climbing with a partner is safer than going alone. At the very least, tell someone where you're going and when you plan to return.

Recommended gear:
boots
hiking poles
water bottles
map
compass
sunglasses (spares are also advised)
sunscreen (the stronger the better)
first aid kit
water filter and/or iodine tablets

Optional items:
ice axe and crampons (for early season outings)
camera
GPS device
Mosquito netting and/or repellant

Mount Maclure. Photo by Dan Johanson

Author's journal of climbing Mount Lyell, 2003:

Climbing up the glacier of Mount Lyell was an adventure unlike any other we had attempted in Yosemite. Six of us donned crampons and started up the ice field, axes in hand. Something about this mountain pulled on my cousin Andy, and he pulled the rest of us along on a brisk October weekend. After a slow but steady ascent of the glacier, we stood beneath the summit block. But there we plainly saw that the final push up Yosemite's highest mountain would be a lot harder than the class 3 scramble the guidebook described...

31 Clouds Rest

Distance: 14.2 miles round trip
Time: 6 to 8 hours
Difficulty: class 3; moderate to strenuous
Parking and trailhead: Sunrise Lakes Trailhead at southwest corner of Tenaya Lake, elevation 8,150 feet
Summit: elevation 9,926 feet
Best season: June through September
Permits: none needed for day use but required for overnight travel; visit Tuolumne Meadows Wilderness Center

Overview

Clouds Rest is Half Dome's overlooked sibling that deserves more attention. Though less distinct than its more famous neighbor, Clouds Rest offers a shorter hike, fewer hikers, and less climbing. The summit delivers a great look down at Half Dome and a breathtaking panoramic view that many consider the best in the park.

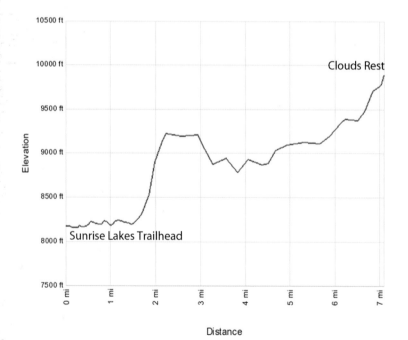

Climbing the climb

Hike east on the Sunrise Lakes Trail beside pine saplings and then across the lake outlet. Early in the season, high water may require hikers to wade across Tenaya Creek. Later in the year you can cross the outlet on stepping stones and the area dries up entirely in fall. The trail turns south and climbs a steep ridge on switchbacks in the second mile, gaining about a thousand feet. This is the hardest part of the hike.

Leveling off, the route reaches a split. To the left and east are the Sunrise Lakes. Stay right for the Forsyth Trail heading south, passing pleasantly through pine trees and skirting a small pond. Soon you will reach another trail junction; stay right for the Clouds Rest Trail, heading southwest.

Next make the memorable final climb up the narrow ridge. Keep your nerve! The exposure is unsettling but the hiking is straightforward.

From the summit, enjoy your view of not just Half Dome but also Basket Dome, Mount Watkins, Mount Conness, Matthes Crest, Triple Divide Peak, Mount Starr King, and much more.

Camping on the summit is not permitted but other camping opportunities abound nearby (a wilderness permit is required). An overnight stay will permit you to see a magnificent sunset and sunrise.

Insider tips

This hike is best enjoyed in late summer or early fall. Snow covers the trail in early season and mosquitoes arrive in force in early summer.

Several streams provide water in the early season but usually dry up by the fall. The trail passes a small pond shortly past the halfway point. To treat its stagnant water, a filter works best.

Instead of hiking out and back, overnight backpackers may like to return on different routes. Below and northeast of the Clouds Rest summit, a connecting trail leads to the John Muir Trail, leading to Yosemite Valley to the southwest or Tuolumne Meadows to the northeast.

Distances and details

Start: Sunrise Lakes Trailhead
0.2 miles: Junction with trail to Tuolumne Meadows (go right)
2.5 miles: Junction with trail to Sunrise Lakes (go right)
4.7 miles: Junction with trail to Yosemite Valley (go right)
7.1 miles: Clouds Rest
14.2 miles: Return to Sunrise Lakes Trailhead

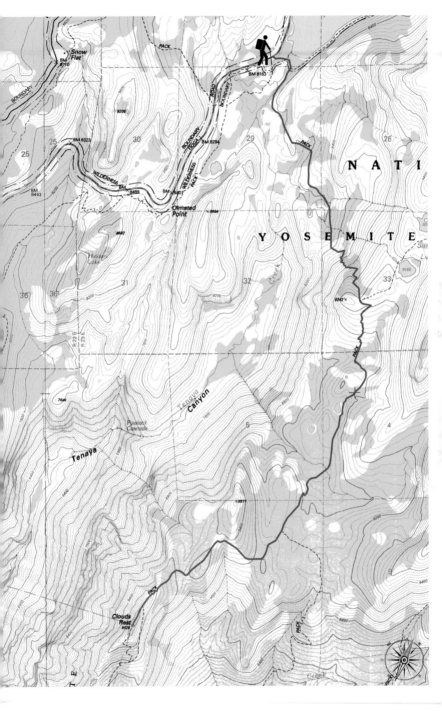

32 Mount Hoffmann

Distance: 6.2 miles round trip
Time: 3 to 5 hours
Difficulty: class 3; moderate
Parking and trailhead: May Lake, elevation 8,860 feet
Summit: elevation 10,850 feet
Best season: June through October
Permits: none needed for day use

Overview

A fairly short climb leads to a grand view of virtually every major peak in Yosemite, with a visit to a beautiful lake as a bonus. Mount Hoffmann provides the best payoff for effort of any mountain in the park. While the route climbs steadily and requires fitness and altitude acclimation, hikers gain only about 2,000 feet from trailhead to summit.

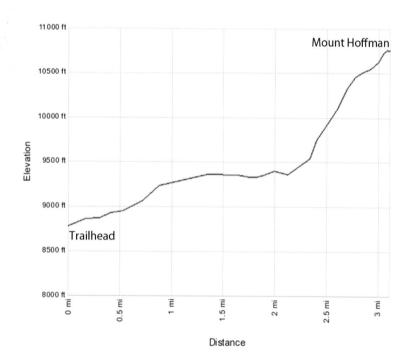

Half Dome and Hoffmann's Thumb are
visible from the summit of Mount Hoffmann.

Climbing the climb

"Go straight to Mount Hoffmann," John Muir once suggested. "From the summit nearly all of the Yosemite Park is displayed like a map." To take his advice, take the May Lake turnoff from Tioga Road, about 2.5 miles east of Olmsted Point. Follow the rough but paved road 1.7 miles to a parking area. Pick up the northbound trail that gains about 500 feet on the way to May Lake at elevation 9,329 feet. Your route arrives at the lake's southeast corner. Proceed west along May Lake's southern shore. At the lake's southwest corner, the trail turns southwest and the climb resumes.

An unofficial and unmaintained route, the summit trail is marked by rock cairns and footprints. While short, the climb ascends steeply, gaining about 1,500 feet in the last mile. Take your time and enjoy more than 100 different varieties of wildflowers growing on the mountainside. The final segment requires some class 3 scrambling up granite slabs.

The summit overlooks mountains too numerous to list in an awesome display. Rock climbers may take interest in Hoffmann's Thumb, a blocky tower near the peak. This is a great place to relax and survey the majesty of Yosemite.

Insider tips

Bring a map, whether or not you use it for the climb, to help identify the dozens of peaks visible from the summit.

If you stop for lunch, keep an eye on your food because there are hungry marmots around here!

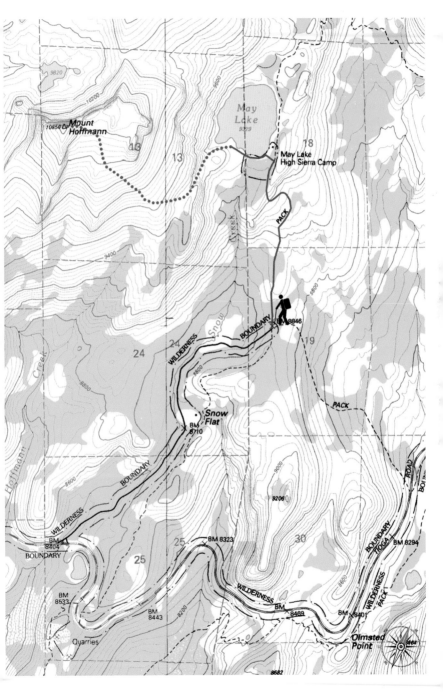

Mount Watkins

Distance: 5 miles round trip
Time: 3 to 5 hours
Difficulty: class 2; moderate
Parking and trailhead: beside Tioga Road 2 miles west of Olmsted Point, elevation 8,540 feet
Summit: elevation 8,490 feet
Best season: June through October
Permits: none needed for day use

Overview

There aren't many mountains with summits lower than their nearest trailheads. This one also boasts a short hike and a magnificent look at Half Dome and Tenaya Canyon. While the approach requires mostly off-trail hiking, the terrain is mild and the route finding is fairly simple. If you're looking for a little-known, rewarding adventure that's not too difficult, look no further.

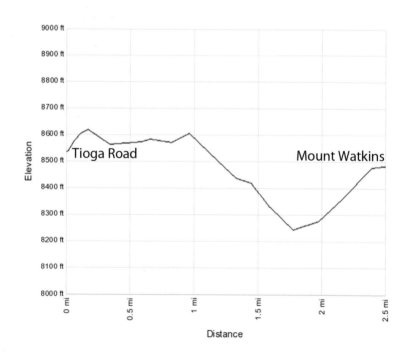

Climbing the climb

Park in a large pullout north of Tioga Road. Hike south across the highway to pick up the southbound trail. Officially it starts near the end of the road's sharp turn but hikers can also take the dirt road leading to a quarry and pick up the trail there. Follow the path south for about a mile until it veers right (west).

Leave the summer trail here and continue hiking downhill to the south on the east slope of the ridge. Your path should cross a small saddle before crossing another official trail from Olmsted Point to Snow Creek.

Proceed further south, off trail, as you begin ascending the north slope of Mount Watkins. The climb only gains about 250 feet from the slope's bottom to the summit. On the way you'll see a ridge extending to a northeast point that may appear to be the summit. Though it's not, you still may enjoy the quarter-mile detour to explore it.

The true summit is about a half mile southwest of the potential turnoff and 150 feet higher. Though the rounded mountaintop lacks a distinct peak, visitors will know they have arrived by the unique look at Half Dome that comes into view.

Retrace your steps to return to Tioga Road.

Insider tips

As you part from the summer trail a mile after the start to descend the ridge, look for winter trail markers on the trees to guide you for about the next mile.

Consider a visit to Snow Creek Cabin, a half mile west of the summit and 800 feet lower. It's closed in summer but will be easier to find in winter if you get acquainted with the area.

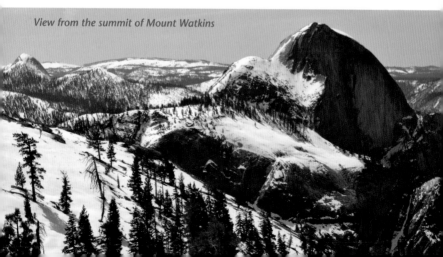

View from the summit of Mount Watkins

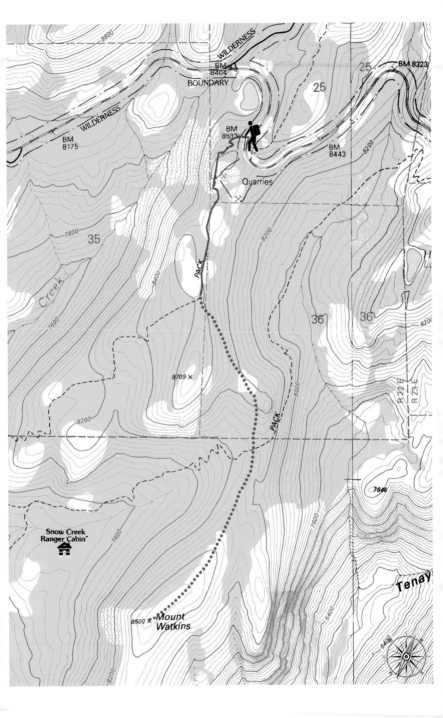

34 Cathedral Peak

Distance: 6 miles round trip
Time: 4 to 6 hours
Difficulty: class 3; moderate to strenuous
Parking and trailhead: beside Tioga Road at Cathedral Lakes Trailhead, elevation 8,585 feet
Summit: elevation 10,912 feet
Best season: June through October
Permits: none needed for day use

Overview

A climbing shrine since John Muir scaled the mountain in 1869, Cathedral Peak is regarded by many as the most beautiful mountain in Tuolumne. Popular among rock climbers, the peak also offers a non-technical yet vigorous hike to its summit area which sports a jaw-dropping view. While the hike is not an officially maintained trail, it's a well-established route that dozens hike daily in summer.

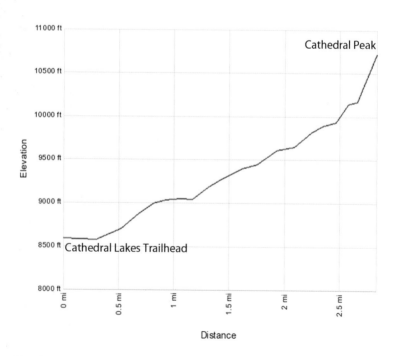

Climbing the climb

Summiting Cathedral Peak may prove a religious experience. At the least, it's a potentially habit-forming activity. If you love Yosemite peaks and are fit enough for a challenging hike, you need to do this one.

From the trailhead on Tioga Road, hike southwest on the John Muir Trail for about half a mile. This uphill segment will take about 10 minutes. Be on the lookout for a well-traveled and sandy use trail that splits from the main route on the left (east) side. Sometimes logs are placed across this turnoff so that John Muir Trail hikers will not get sidetracked. Your path is 3 feet wide and will quickly parallel the west side of Budd Creek. Follow the trail leading southwest and uphill toward the mountain.

Eventually the trail splits into multiple paths headed for Cathedral's southeast face. Before getting there, cut west through trees to climb to the more gradual east face. Ascend the sandy switchbacks to the summit area; this will take a while. Then worship on the granite shrine before retracing your steps.

Insider tips

To reach the top of the actual summit block requires about 15 feet of class 5 rock climbing, climbing gear, and rope. Save this challenge for another day if you're not equipped and qualified.

Looking west from the summit area, spot Eichorn Pinnacle and the Cathedral Lakes, which make for great pictures.

Summit of Cathedral Peak

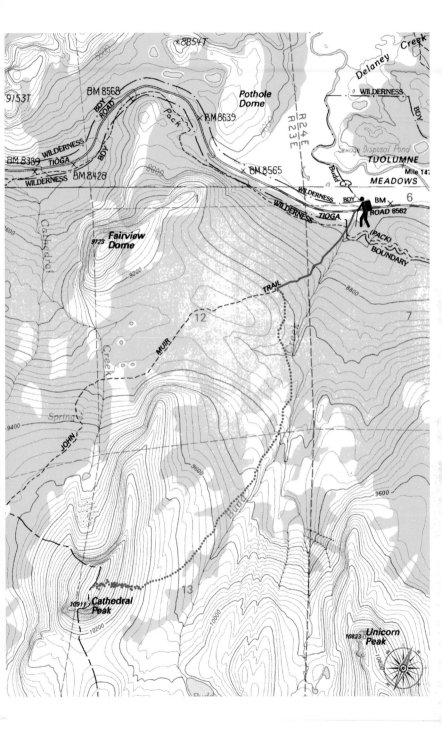

Half Dome

Distance: 16.4 miles round trip
Time: 8 to 12 hours
Difficulty: class 3; strenuous
Parking: Curry Village or Yosemite Village day lot (take the free shuttle to Happy Isles)
Trailhead: Happy Isles, elevation 4,000 feet
Summit: elevation 8,839 feet
Best season: June through September
Permits: required; see page 184

Overview

The most iconic mountain in Yosemite commands a powerful view and an incomparable appeal, and you don't have to be a climbing expert to ascend the steel cables to its summit. Because of crowding, the park has limited the number of hikers and required permits in recent years. These regulations have increased the planning required but have also improved the experience, making it safer and more enjoyable. For many, reaching the peak is a lifetime outdoors highlight.

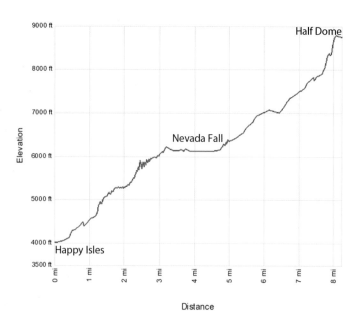

Climbing the climb

Take one look at Half Dome and you'll feel its magnetic pull, but make sure you're physically ready before lacing up your boots. That goes for any outdoors adventure but it warrants special mention here. Even with permit requirements and limits in place, Half Dome attracts tens of thousands of hikers per season, many of them more ambitious than prepared to ascend nearly 5,000 feet. Hundreds suffer difficulties from exhaustion to serious injuries and need assistance every summer. Please do yourself (and the search and rescue team) a favor by training for your experience. This should not be your first tiring hike at high elevation.

The hike officially begins at Happy Isles. Private automobiles may not drive there so most people park at Curry Village and either walk about a mile or take the free shuttle bus. Make sure you cross the bridge before turning starting up the John Muir Trail. After crossing the footbridge, you'll soon reach a split between the Mist and John Muir trails. You may choose

Summit of Half Dome

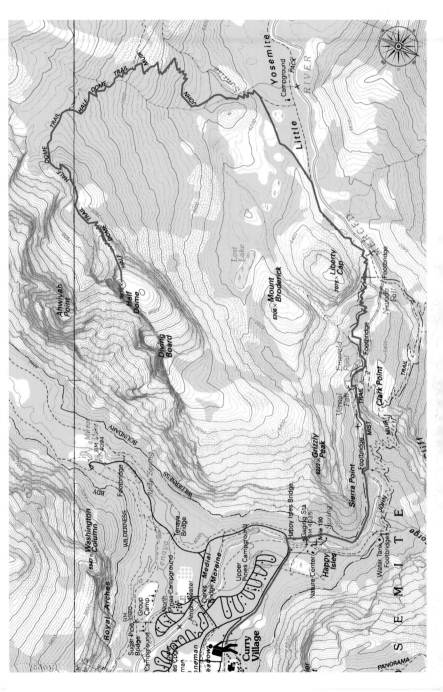

either one; the trails rejoin in a few miles. The Mist Trail is shorter, steeper, wetter and gives a great close-up of Vernal Fall. The Muir will be less crowded.

Both of the trails cross the Merced River on footbridges and the two paths rejoin in the shadow of Liberty Cap. Continue northeast to a split in the trail. To the right is Little Yosemite Valley and the backpacking campground. To the left is the route to Half Dome. After about a mile and 1,000 feet of elevation gain, the trail splits again. This time you turn left to leave the Muir and continue the ascent on the Half Dome Trail.

After checking in with the ranger beneath the subdome, climb about 600 steps atop the mountain's shoulder. Now it's time for the main event. The cables up Half Dome's northeast face steeply climb 200 yards. If you brought gloves, put them on here. Take a last look for storm clouds, and if you see any, turn around. Otherwise, start the climb. Soon you'll summit the most picturesque mountain in the park. Make sure you enjoy the awesome view before heading back.

Insider tips

Take a pair of gloves, which will save your skin and spare you pain going up and down the cables. Many hikers now wear climbing harnesses and use slings and carabiners to tether themselves to the cables for added safety.

Half Dome can attract lightning, and the summit is a potentially deadly place to be in a thunderstorm. If dark clouds threaten, go back. Don't worry about "wasting" your permit.

Start early! This will maximize your chance of reaching the summit and avoiding afternoon storms.

Distances and details

Start: Happy Isles
0.9 miles: Vernal Fall Bridge
1.0 miles: Junction of Mist Trail and John Muir Trail
1.6 miles: Top of Vernal Fall (via Mist Trail)
3.5 miles: Top of Nevada Fall (via Mist Trail)
4.1 miles: Junction with trail to Little Yosemite Valley (go left)
6.0 miles: Junction with Half Dome trail and John Muir Trail (go left)
8.2 miles: Half Dome summit
16.4 miles: Return to Happy Isles

Getting a Half Dome Permit

Permits are required every day during the summer season while Half Dome's cables are up, normally mid-May to mid-October. The park allots 300 per day, with 225 for day hikers and 75 for overnight backpackers.

Day hiker permits are first made available through a lottery in March. You can apply through recreation.gov for a group of up to six people; results are announced in early April. Alternatively, day hikers may enter a daily permit lottery two days ahead of a planned hiking date. About 20 percent of daily lottery entries are successful. There's a $4.50 charge to enter either lottery, and if you get a permit, there's an additional charge of $8 per hiker.

Backpackers, with the wilderness permits required for overnight backcountry travel, apply for Half Dome permits separately. The park allows wilderness permit reservations up to 24 weeks in advance through fax, phone, or mail. See details at the nps.gov page for Yosemite wilderness permit reservations. Check the Half Dome box on your request. Reserved permits cost $5, plus $5 per person in the group.

Backpackers without reservations may request wilderness permits and Half Dome permits at the park's wilderness centers starting at 11:00 AM, one day prior to departure. Like day hikers, backpackers pay $8 per person for Half Dome permits if they are available.

All Half Dome permits are non-transferable and a ranger will check photo identification below the mountain's subdome. Scalpers made this requirement necessary by purchasing large numbers of permits and reselling them for greatly inflated prices during the first years of the program.

Note that the park's permitting procedures are subject to change; check nps.gov for the latest details.

Mount Dana

Distance: 5.8 miles round trip
Time: 4 to 6 hours
Difficulty: class 2; strenuous
Parking: beside the road near Tioga Pass or in the lot beside park entrance buildings
Trailhead: Tioga Pass, elevation 9,943 feet
Summit: 13,057 feet elevation
Best season: June through October
Permits: none required

Overview

Mount Dana offers a rewarding high-elevation climbing experience with a minimum of time, gear, and expertise required. A fit hiker setting out from Tioga Pass can reach the second-highest summit in Yosemite and return in half a day. An unmarked but fairly clear trail leads across Dana Meadows and up the rocky west face of the mountain. Snow can make route finding tricky in the early season.

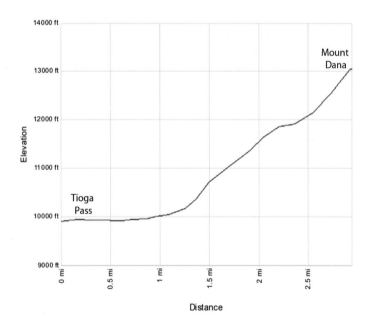

Climbing the climb

Pick up the path leading east from the park entrance kiosk; there's no trail sign. Your route leads through Dana Meadows, where a colorful variety of wildflowers grow after snow melts in the early season.

Past the meadows, the trail becomes rocky, the climb steepens, and switchbacks begin. The climb flattens at a plateau around 11,500 feet, the elevation midpoint between Tioga Pass and the summit. There's little vegetation and no granite here; welcome to a world of metamorphic rock.

From here a number of use paths lead to the peak. The preferred and most-used route runs close to the ridgeline. Increasingly the climb becomes a scramble up a rocky slope until you reach the summit.

Mount Dana's summit provides majestic views of Mono Lake, Tuolumne Meadows, and the spiny backbone of the Sierra Nevada range. Enjoy the panoramic view that's among the best in the Sierra Nevada before descending.

Insider tips

Though its summit hike is fairly short, Mount Dana's high elevation means most climbers will need to acclimate a few days to ascend comfortably. An attempt on the same day as a drive from sea level is a recipe for a splitting headache.

In the early season, snow provides a mixed blessing. It can complicate route finding but also permits glissading, provided hikers are equipped with ice axes and crampons. Make sure you're also properly skilled in recognizing suitable conditions and terrain: look for soft snow and gentle slopes and avoid icy snow and steep slopes, especially that drop into boulders.

View from summit of Mount Dana

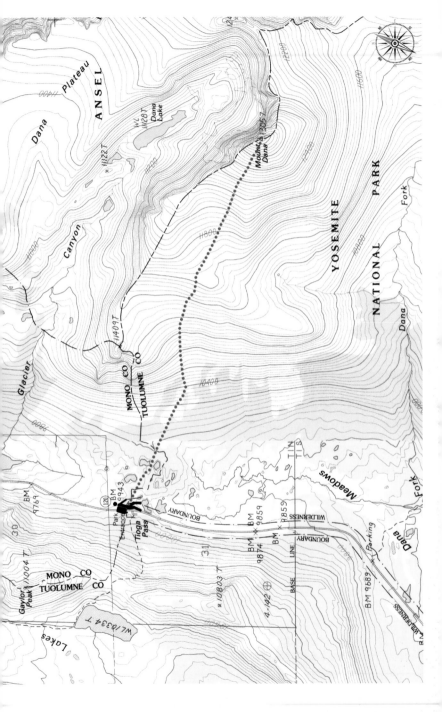

A climber enjoys the view from the summit of Mount Dana.

Mount Conness

Distance: 8 miles round trip
Time: 6 to 8 hours
Difficulty: class 3; moderate to strenuous
Parking: beside Saddlebag Road outside Sawmill Campground (the lot is for registered campers only)
Trailhead: Sawmill Campground, elevation 9,842 feet
Summit: elevation 12,590 feet
Best season: July through September
Permits: none needed for day use

Overview

There's more than one way to climb a high Sierra peak like Mount Conness, which offers great high-altitude rock climbing. But you can also hike through the Inyo National Forest up the mountain's eastern slope to one of the highest summits in Yosemite. This climb requires stamina, route-finding skills, and an ascent of class 3 terrain with intimidating exposure near the summit.

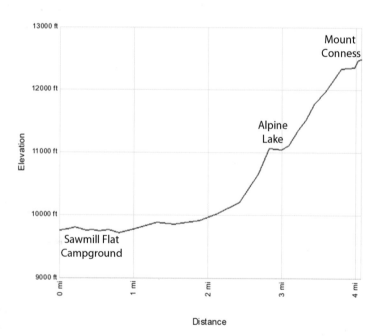

Climbing the climb

Hike around Tuolumne Meadows long enough and you're bound to see towering Mount Conness, the highest Sierra Nevada summit north of Tioga Road. If it calls to you, consider taking a closer look.

From Highway 120 about 2 miles east of Tioga Pass, drive north on gravely Saddlebag Lake Road 1.6 miles to Sawmill Campground. Park beside the road and walk through the camp. The trail continues past the camp beside Lee Vining Creek into a pine-filled valley beneath the eastern flank of Mount Conness. As you pass the Carnegie Institute research hut, enjoy the bubbling stream and wildflowers which fill the grassy meadow on your way to steeper terrain.

The path becomes less clear as you climb above the tree line and onto the mountain's rocky eastern shoulder. In fact, you may not see a path at all, especially in the early season before the snow melts. Keep heading west and gaining elevation to reach Alpine Lake; drink and refill water bottles here. As you continue climbing, the Conness Lakes and Conness Glacier come into view near the summit plateau. You may see some marmots.

From the plateau you will finally spot the summit atop a rocky bulge. To reach it requires scrambling up a narrow arete above steep and long drops on either side. The exposure demands careful attention and may cause anxiety, especially among those uninitiated to rock climbing. This class 3 segment is the crux of the climb.

At the summit, catch your breath and enjoy the rewarding view, which includes Mount Ritter, Banner Peak, Mount Lyell, and Mount Maclure to the south. If this adventure inspires you to return on one of the mountain's technical climbs, now you know the most common descent, which is the route you just completed in reverse. Take it to return to Sawmill Campground.

Insider tips

Although climbing Mount Conness requires less elevation gain than many other mountains, its high starting point and summit will leave flatlanders gasping for air. Acclimate for a while before trying this one and consider taking some aspirin or ibuprofen along.

A peak this high has plenty of snow in the early season; plan accordingly.

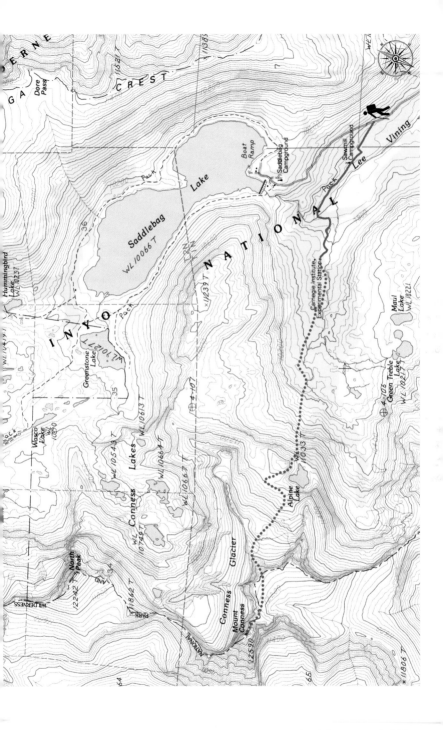

38 Amelia Earhart Peak

Distance: 17 miles round trip
Time: 8 to 12 hours
Difficulty: class 3; moderate to strenuous
Parking and trailhead: Tuolumne Meadows Wilderness Center, elevation 8,680 feet
Summit: elevation 11,974 feet
Best season: June through October
Permits: none needed for day use but required for overnight travel; visit Tuolumne Meadows Wilderness Center

Overview

This adventure starts on the John Muir Trail through Lyell Canyon. The trip becomes more challenging where hikers go off-trail to traverse the west ridge of Potter Point, gradually climbing to the notch beneath Amelia Earhart Peak. There is no maintained or visible trail for the final 2 miles where the ascent requires scrambling and route-finding skills but the climb is fairly straightforward.

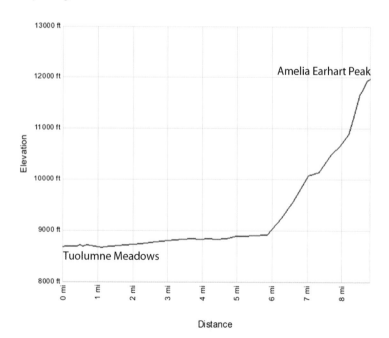

Climbing the climb

Climb high into the mountain air at Amelia Earhart Peak but navigate carefully to avoid disappearing like the famed aviator.

At the Tuolumne Meadows Wilderness Center, pick up the John Muir Trail heading east through a meadow and past the rangers' office. Following the signs for Donohue Pass, cross a bridge over the Lyell Fork of the Tuolumne River, which will be your companion for the next 5 miles.

When you see the prominent Potter Point, keep an eye out for the junction with the trail to Ireland Lake. Here's where things get interesting. Start up the trail to Ireland Lake and climb toward a saddle. Within a mile, you will have to go off-trail, cross Ireland Creek, and ascend Potter Point's west ridge toward Amelia Earhart Peak, which will come into view as you climb, to the south of Potter Point. There is no clear trail though you may find footprints. Your main goal should be to gain elevation as you draw closer to the mountain. As you approach, you will see a notch between the ridge and the north face of the peak; aim for it. From here, scramble south over granite slabs about a quarter mile to the summit. Retrace your steps to return.

Insider tips

Because this trip involves off-trail hiking and scrambling, a single hiker who became hurt might wait a long time for someone to happen by. Tell someone where you're going and when you plan to return.

This makes for a long haul in one day, especially if you recently arrived at high altitude. Consider an overnight trip.

Distances and details

Start: Tuolumne Meadows Wilderness Center
1.8 miles: Junction with trail to Tuolumne Pass and Vogelsang (go left)
6 miles: Junction with trail to Ireland Lake (stay left)
8.5 miles: Amelia Earhart Peak
17 miles: Return to Tuolumne Meadows Wilderness Center

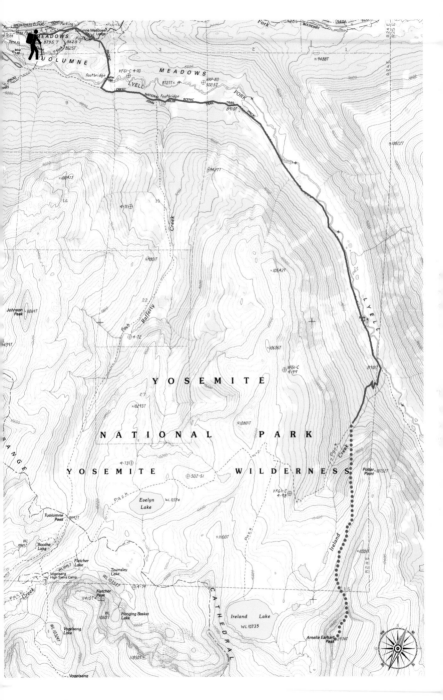

*View from the summit of
Amelia Earhart Peak*

Matterhorn Peak

39

Distance: 10 miles round trip
Time: 6 to 10 hours
Difficulty: class 3; strenuous
Parking: use the private lot in Mono Village, 15 miles east of Bridgeport
Trailhead: Horse Creek, elevation 7,092 feet
Summit: elevation 12,279 feet
Best season: June through October
Permits: none needed for day use but required for overnight trips; visit the Forest Service office on Highway 395, 1 mile south of Bridgeport

Overview

Matterhorn Peak appears steep and formidable and its impressive summit commands attention from miles around. Named after the famous peak straddling Switzerland and Italy, Yosemite's Matterhorn attracts mountaineers to its glacier and worthy rock climbing routes but also features a non-technical trail to a rewarding peak. A 5,187-foot elevation gain makes this physically demanding, but the trek from trailhead to summit is just 5 miles.

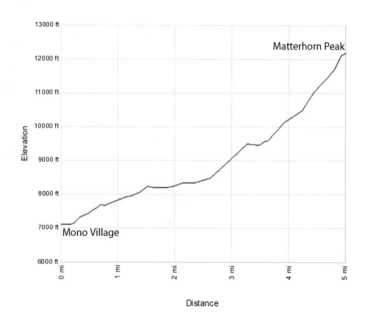

Climbing the climb

Matterhorn Peak provides climbers a taste of high-altitude adventure. Yet the trek's rapid elevation gain and rocky terrain make it a physical challenge not to be underestimated.

Starting from the backpackers' parking lot, locate the trailhead in the southeast corner of the RV area. Cross a wooden bridge over a creek and continue south to the Horse Creek Trail bulletin board. Hike up switchbacks beside the creek and through wooded terrain. After about 45 minutes, you will reach Horse Creek Meadow at 8,000 feet, followed by a trail sign and junction. Instead of Cattle Creek Trail heading east, stay on the less-trodden Horse Creek Trail heading south.

Now the route becomes a use trail through gravel and boulders. Stay on the left (east) side of Horse Creek. This would be a good place to refill water bottles; eventually the water runs only beneath the rocks. Enjoy the willows and early-season waterfalls. Hikers ascend a false pass before spotting and climbing over the true Horse Creek Pass. Several variations are possible; when in doubt, stay close to the creek.

Now only a short stretch of class 2 and 3 scrambling stands between you and the summit. The gentlest route climbs Matterhorn's southeast slope.

From the peak on a clear day, you'll see entrancing views of the Mokolumne Wilderness to the north, the Sweetwater mountains to the east, Tower Peak to the west, and Yosemite's Mount Dana, Mount Conness, and Clouds Rest to the south. Enjoy them before retracing your steps.

Insider tips

Visitors in the early season should expect to find snow in the gullies and near the summit; hikers should take crampons and ice axes and know how to self-arrest.

Glissading may speed the descent from the summit and add an element of fun in the early season, provided climbers are equipped with ice axes and crampons. Make sure you're also properly skilled in recognizing suitable conditions and terrain: look for soft snow and gentle slopes and avoid icy snow and steep slopes, especially that drop into boulders.

Overnight visitors can find camping opportunities in Horse Creek Meadow and beyond Horse Creek Pass.

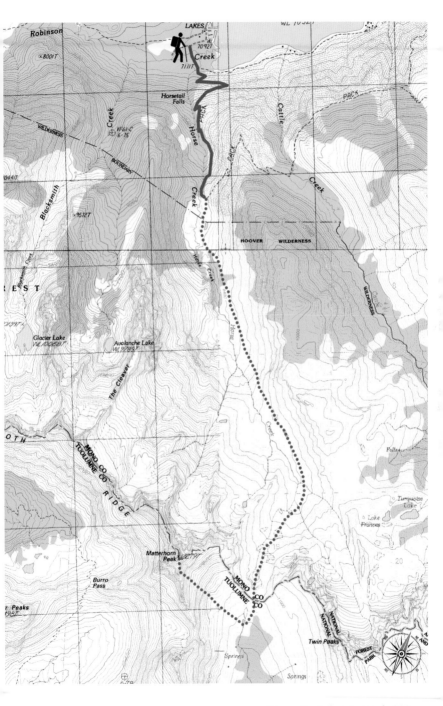

Mount Lyell

Distance: 25 miles round trip
Time: 2 to 3 days
Difficulty: class 3; strenuous
Parking and trailhead: Tuolumne Meadows Wilderness Center, elevation 8,680 feet
Summit: elevation 13,114 feet
Best season: July through September
Permits: none needed for day use but required for overnight travel; visit Tuolumne Meadows Wilderness Center

Overview

The tallest mountain in Yosemite, Mount Lyell is the longest and most difficult climb in this guide. It's also the most rewarding challenge and perhaps the greatest adventure. Much of the journey involves simply hiking in Lyell Canyon. Near Donohue Pass, climbers leave the John Muir Trail and ascend the mountain's northern drainage. The final push requires class 3 and possibly class 4 rock climbing.

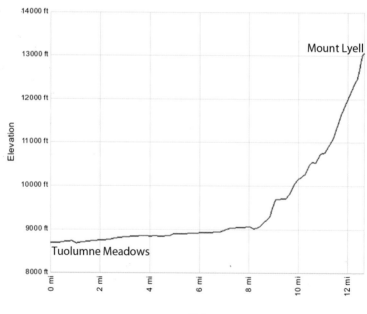

Climbing the climb

While some complete this adventure in a day, most take two or three days. This is a big one and it's not a race. Set aside enough time to do it right.

At Tuolumne Meadows Wilderness Center, pick up the John Muir Trail heading east through a meadow and past the rangers' office (see map on page 139). Following signs for Donohue Pass, cross a bridge over the Lyell Fork of the Tuolumne River. Hike south on the Muir beside the river for several miles to the end of Lyell Canyon.

Next the trail climbs toward Donohue Pass and the real work begins. From the start of the climb, the trail crosses over a bridge in about a mile. Many switchbacks later, the southbound trail turns sharply east toward Donohue Pass. Instead, leave the Muir and continue south up the mountain's drainage. Hike up the granite canyon beside a creek as you climb above the tree line.

When Lyell comes into view, climbers have a choice. Some climb up the glacier to the mountain's east arete and scramble up rock to the summit; this is the most direct route and will require ice axes and crampons. Others aim for the Lyell-Maclure saddle and ascend up talus on the mountain's northwest ridge. This is longer but more moderate. Your level of experience, gear, and snow conditions should all factor into your choice. This guide's map illustrates the northwest ridge approach.

Savor a hardest-earned summit in Yosemite and the king-of-the-world view. Retrace your steps to your base camp and Tuolumne Meadows.

Insider tips

A big snow year and early-season outing mean safer and easier climbing near the summit. The opposite is also true. After a dry winter, climbers will encounter loose rock and class 4 terrain.

Take an ice axe and crampons. If you leave them behind, you are sure to want them.

Don't wait too long to climb Mount Lyell, because its glacier is shrinking.

Distances and details

Start: Tuolumne Meadows Wilderness Center
1.8 miles: Junction with trail to Tuolumne Pass and Vogelsang (go left)
6 miles: Junction with trail to Ireland Lake (stay left)
10.2 miles: Bridge
12.5 miles: Mount Lyell
25 miles: Return to Tuolumne Meadows Wilderness Center

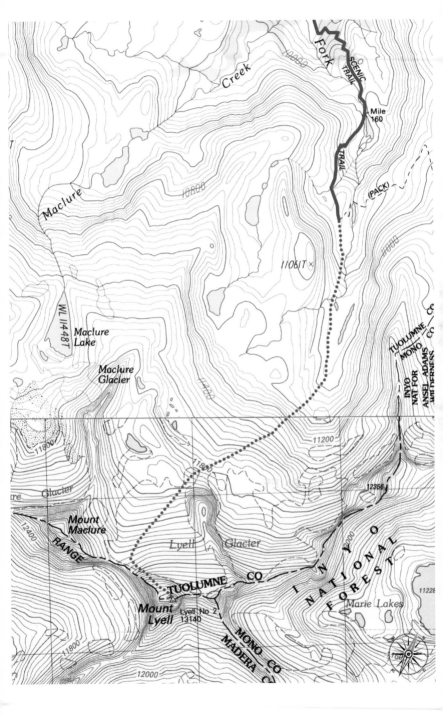

Climbers reach the summit of Eichorn Pinnacle.

Rock Climbing

Introduction to Rock Climbing

Though Yosemite offers nearly infinite possibilities for skiers, hikers, backpackers, and peak baggers, nothing sets the park apart from other Sierra Nevada destinations as much as its rock climbing. Enormous and exquisite granite walls, peaks, spires, and domes demand attention throughout Yosemite Valley and Tuolumne Meadows. Limitless challenges abound for climbers of all ability levels. Take a walk through Camp 4 and you'll meet kindred spirits from all over the world; many who discover adventure here feel the urge to return for the rest of their lives.

More than other activities described in this guide, rock climbing requires specialized skills and no small amount of gear. Many excellent manuals explain such things as placing gear, building anchors, rappelling, jamming, and smearing, though this book does not and could not do so without doubling in length. Rather, this guide aims to provide a path for novice climbers with some abilities (like tying into a rope and belaying) and a minimal amount of gear (such as shoes, harnesses, belay devices, rope, and carabiners) to expand their skills and experiences on suitable Yosemite climbs. The introductory information in this chapter will help beginners understand and use this book for that purpose.

Climbers in Yosemite and elsewhere use a rating system to define and describe terrain. Class 5 indicates rock climbing requiring gear, ropes, and belays for protection. These climbs are also rated with a second numeral that specifies their difficulty. Climbs rated from 5.0 to 5.6 are suitable for beginners. Routes from 5.7 to 5.9 are intermediate. Only experts should attempt climbs rated 5.10 and higher. This is known as the Yosemite Decimal System, which climbers use throughout the United States.

The climbs described in this book range from 5.0 to 5.10, with an emphasis on routes rated 5.6 and 5.7. In general, the climbs are ordered from shortest to longest, from those requiring little gear to those requiring more and from easiest to hardest in difficulty. Climbs at the first three destinations can be top-roped without a lead. Next are several single-pitch climbs which require leading, and last are three multi-pitch routes.

Each outing described includes a list of necessary skills and needed gear. At a minimum, climbers must know how to tie into a rope, set an anchor and climb, and belay a top-roped pitch for each of the routes. Shoes, harnesses, belay devices, carabiners, rope, and helmets are needed for all of the climbs, and some of them will require quickdraws, slings, nuts, and cams. A 60-meter rope is strongly recommended; only a few of these climbs can be done with a 50-meter rope.

While the park requires no permits for rock climbing, please remember that it is a dangerous pursuit. Learn to place gear and build anchors properly. Exercise great caution while leading and rappelling; most climbing accidents (and fatalities) occur during these activities. Always back up gear placements and anchors. Always wear a helmet. Be vigilant when climbing beneath another party which could drop gear or dislodge rocks onto you. Know that Yosemite's excellent search and rescue team provides services only as a last resort. All climbers are responsible for their own safety.

Most new climbers learn from friends or others who already possess both experience and gear. You may enjoy your outdoor climbing more after learning some of the basics in a gym. Consider taking a class through Yosemite Mountaineering School. However you get started, climb safely and enjoy your discoveries in the greatest rock climbing mecca in the world.

Climbing Maps Legend

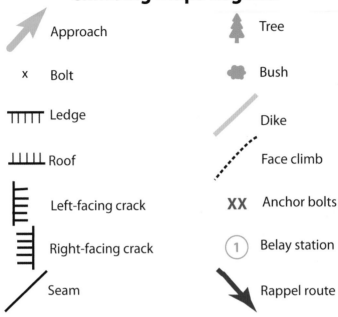

↗	Approach	🌲	Tree
x	Bolt	🌳	Bush
TTTTT	Ledge	╱	Dike
⊥⊥⊥⊥	Roof	⌐	Face climb
	Left-facing crack	XX	Anchor bolts
	Right-facing crack	①	Belay station
/	Seam	↘	Rappel route

Rock Climbing Glossary

anchor: a secure gear arrangement on a climb used to protect belay stations

belay: to protect a climber from falling by managing and securing the rope

bolt: a metal anchor placed in rock for climbing protection

cam: a spring-loaded climbing protection device that wedges into rock cracks

carabiners: metal rings with spring-loaded gates used to direct and secure rope

clean: to remove gear from a climb

chimney: a vertical rock shaft

crag: a conveniently accessible climbing area

crux: the most difficult part of a particular climb

dihedral: a rock corner

jam: to wedge hands or feet into a crack in the process of climbing

lead (n): a climber's effort to ascend rock while placing protection en route

lead (v): to ascend rock while placing protection

lieback: a climbing technique using hands to pull rock features while feet push simultaneously

nut: a climbing protection device with a metal piece attached to a wire that wedges into rock cracks

pitch: a unit of climbing distance usually up to one rope length long

pro, protection: climbing gear used to protect against falls or to assist in upward progress

quickdraw: a pair of carabiners connected by a sling

rappel (n): a descent on a secure rope

rap, rappel (v): to descend on a secure rope

runner: a sling used with carabiners to connect climbing protection to a rope

run out, runout: a climbing effort with long spaces between gear placements, increasing the length of a potential fall

smear: a climbing technique using friction to hold feet on smooth or featureless rock

spot: for a belayer to protect a lead climber from falling with hands low on a pitch

stem: to climb between two rock features using opposing pressure from hands or feet

traverse: to climb laterally

top-rope: to climb with an anchor and rope already established above for protection

Author's journal of climbing Half Dome's Snake Dike, 1999:

Clinging to a nearly blank wall of granite, I took a deep breath and tried to stay calm. I had told Morry that we'd climb this route, just 5.7, without a problem. Yet I'd drifted off-route onto much harder rock, 20 feet above my last gear, and all bets were off. Some climbers don't mind long leader-falls but I've never been one of them. Spotting my wrong turn, I put my head down and slowly traversed back to the route on dime-thin fingertip holds, saying a quiet hallelujah when I finally clipped another bolt. Morry made the pitch look a lot easier than I did. That day we learned that overcoming a challenge or two along the way makes reaching the top more exhilarating.

Pothole Dome

Area: Tuolumne Meadows
Difficulty: 5.0 to 5.10, with plenty of choices in between
Parking: beside Tioga Road at Pothole Dome at the west edge of Tuolumne Meadows
Best season: May through October

Overview

Here's the best area in the park for beginners. A short walk leads to six long single-pitch routes, all with anchor bolts and suitable for top-roping.

Skills needed

Climbers will need to tie into a rope, build an anchor with bolts, climb pitches rated 5.0 and above, and belay a top-roped pitch.

Gear needed

Take helmets, harnesses, shoes, belay devices, locking carabiners, long slings, and a 60-meter rope.

Approach

Follow the nature trail as it loops around the west end of the meadow and cut left into the trees when you first reach the dome. Looking west, you should see Family Fun, Slippery When Dry, and You Found It, and an easy scramble to the bolts above the routes is right in front of you.

To reach Christmas Tree, Pick Your Poison, and Wolverine Was Here, hike up and over the hill for about a quarter mile. The routes overlook a small pond and you can scramble to the anchors from their left or right sides.

1. Christmas Tree (5.1 to 5.6)

This climb begins beside a pine tree that would look great with ornaments and presents. Your gift is a choice of blocky friction climbs. Directly beneath the anchor is 5.6, and easier climbing is found to the left and right.

2. Pick Your Poison (5.1 to 5.10)

Where else can you find such a wide range of difficulties on the same pitch? On the far left is a water streak rated 5.10. Closer but still left of the anchor is a casual 5.1 stroll. Beneath the anchor is a 5.9 bulge and right of that is a 5.5 variation over a block.

3. Wolverine Was Here (5.0 to 5.4)

Shortest of these climbs, this route begins beside a dead tree that looks like the X-Man Wolverine slashed it with his claws. Hang left for the 5.4 variation or climb straight up under the anchor for 5.0.

Christmas Tree (1), Pick Your Poison (2) and Wolverine Was Here (3).

4. Family Fun (5.0 to 5.8)

Here's a good pitch for families. Kids will like the short walk and the easy knobs. Climb up the far left for junior's first climb, 5.0 friction. Mom and Dad can have a 5.8 date on the face climb right beneath the anchor. To the right are 5.3 and 5.4 climbs with good knobs and smearing for junior's older siblings.

5. Slippery When Dry (5.6 to 5.10)

Glacier-polished granite as smooth as glass makes this a fun challenge. Veer left for the 5.6 variation. Straight beneath the anchors, through the center of the polished granite to a steeper face with fingernail edges, is 5.10. On the right is a 5.9 option that can also lead to the rightmost anchor of You Found It.

6. You Found It (5.1 to 5.9)

Though noted last on this left-to-right list, it's the first route climbers walking over from Tioga Road are likely to see. The 5.9 variation on the left could also lead to the anchor for Slippery When Dry. Stay straight beneath the anchor for a 5.1 warm-up that avoids the polished granite. Hang right for a 5.6 ascent.

Descent

Lower climbers from the anchors and scramble to the bolts to retrieve gear. Christmas Tree, Pick Your Poison, and Wolverine Was Here each have rappel rings.

Insider tips

As the routes run 80 feet to 110 feet, a belayer will have to scramble partway up the base.

The bolts atop Christmas Tree, Pick Your Poison, and Wolverine Was here have rappel rings. The bolts atop Family Fun, Slippery When Dry, and You Found It do not.

Family Fun (4), Slippery When Dry (5) and You Found It (6).

Amy and Chris Kinnney climb at Pothole Dome.

Puppy Dome: Puppy Crack

Area: Tuolumne Meadows
Difficulty: 5.7
Parking: Tuolumne Meadows Wilderness Center
Best season: May through October

Overview

A short approach and easy top-rope make this a popular route for beginners. Finger and hand jams are the key to this steep, short crack.

Skills needed

Climbers will need to tie into a rope, build an anchor using a tree, climb a 5.7 pitch, and belay a top-roped pitch. If leading, climbers will need to place gear in a crack and belay a lead.

Gear needed

Take helmets, harnesses, shoes, belay devices, locking carabiners, slings, and a rope 50 meters or longer. If leading, bring a set of nuts, about five quickdraws and cams from .5 inches to 3 inches.

Approach

Puppy Dome is southwest of the Tuolumne Meadows Wilderness Center parking lot. Locate a trail near the bear lockers leading into the trees to the dome. Proceed counterclockwise around the dome until you spot an obvious vertical crack above a dead tree.

Puppy Crack (5.7)

Scramble up to the left of the climb to reach the trees above the crack. Use slings around one or more of the upper trees to build your anchor. Jamming with fingers, hands and feet will come into play while climbing this fun pitch. Practice crack-climbing technique with the security of a top rope here.

Descent

Scamper down the side, reversing your steps from the scramble to set the anchor.

Insider tips

Please do not anchor to the young tree growing lowest in the crack, which is too small to safely secure a top rope.

This pitch also provides an opportunity to practice placing gear with the security of a top rope.

Swan Slab: West Slabs

Area: Yosemite Valley
Difficulty: 5.1 to 5.8
Parking: Camp 4 (day use area)
Best season: all year

Overview

This is one of the only places in Yosemite where climbers can ascend multiple routes without leading a pitch, making an ideal setting for beginners.

Skills needed

Climbers will need to tie into a rope, build an anchor using a tree and gear, climb pitches from 5.1 up to 5.8, and belay a top-roped pitch.

Gear needed

Take helmets, harnesses, shoes, belay devices, locking carabiners, slings, medium-sized nuts or cams, and a rope 50 meters or longer.

Approach

Swan Slab lies on the north side of Yosemite Valley between Camp 4 and Lower Yosemite Falls. From Camp 4, walk east through the meadow north of the road. In a few moments, the West Slabs will be the first part of the crag that you reach.

West Slabs (5.1 to 5.8)

Climbers can lead the right crack (5.1) by slinging its tree and adding gear if desired. Most simply scramble up the left side to set a top rope. Use the tree atop the rock for the anchor, but back it up with gear in the nearby crack. Practice smearing and face-climbing on the rock's main face, which is harder than it looks and good preparation for longer and more committing Yosemite climbs.

Descent

Scamper down the west side, reversing your steps from the scramble to set the anchor.

Insider tips

Use a long sling in the anchor; this will permit you to use it for several climbs.

To beat crowds, climb early or late in the day, especially on weekends.

Knob Hill: Sloth Wall

Area: Yosemite Valley
Difficulty: 5.7
Parking: beside Big Oak Flat Road at Cascade Creek
Best season: all year

Overview

Cracks and knobs abound on this long and fun pitch. With modest gear requirements and a short crux that's easily protected, the climb provides a good lead for beginners.

Skills needed

Climbers will need to tie into a rope, build an anchor using a tree, lead a 5.7 pitch, belay a lead pitch, and rappel.

Gear needed

Take helmets, harnesses, shoes, belay devices, locking carabiners, long slings, eight quickdraws, a set of nuts, cams from .25 inches to 2.5 inches wide, and at least one 60-meter rope; a second 60-meter rope will make for a somewhat easier descent.

Approach

Park at a pullout beside Big Oak Flat Road east of Cascade Creek, 8 miles east of the Crane Flat gas station or 1.8 miles west from the valley turnoff onto Big Oak Flat Road. Locate a trail north of the road and east of the lower bridge over Cascade Creek. Follow it uphill for 5 minutes. Pot Belly is the first formation; Sloth Wall is above it to the right.

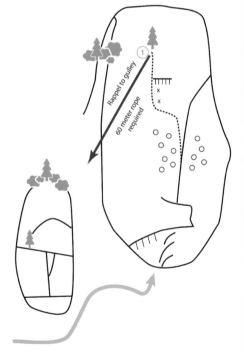

Knob Hill: Sloth Wall (5.7)

Rappel to gulley

60 meter rope required

Sloth Wall (5.7)

The lower segment follows cracks to the right and over a flake, which is the crux. Then the route ascends a sea of knobs as it leans left. Aim for the pine tree and watch for bolts on the upper half.

Descent

With one 60-meter rope, rappel from the tree to the west (left as you face the wall) into a gully. With two 60-meter ropes, use both to rappel to the base.

Insider tips

Use long slings on the bottom of the pitch to reduce rope drag.

Climbers can ascend a second pitch to the top of the formation, though most do not because the best climbing comes on the first pitch.

45 Bunny Slopes

Area: Tuolumne Meadows
Difficulty: 5.6 to 5.9
Parking: beside Tioga Road at Pywiack Dome
Best season: May through October

Overview

Get a feel for Tuolumne slab climbing on five bolted routes within a
10-minute walk of Tioga Road. The climbs are all at least 130 feet long; two
ropes will be needed to top-rope and rappel them.

Matt Johanson climbs Black Diamond.
Photo by Linnae Johansson

Skills needed
Climbers will need to tie into a rope, lead pitches rated at least 5.6, belay a lead pitch, build an anchor using bolts and rappel.

Gear needed
Take helmets, harnesses, shoes, belay devices, locking carabiners, slings, six quickdraws, and two 60-meter ropes. Some pitches take nuts and cams from .5 inches to 2 inches wide.

Approach
Park beside Tioga Road at Pywiack Dome, either a mile east of Tenaya Lake or about 6 miles west of the Tuolumne store and grill. Spot the crag north of the road and hike up the rocky hillside toward it. The best approach leads right (east) to a ledge and then sharply left (west) along the ledge to the base of the crag.

1. Wild in the Streaks (5.7)
The crux comes early on this long pitch up small edges leading to a sea of knobs. This climb shares anchor bolts with Black Diamond.

2. Black Diamond (5.9)
Long and scary 5.9 runouts make this a lead for experts only, as the name suggests. Top-rope this worthy challenge after leading Wild in the Streaks. Near the top is a horizontal crack that takes cams up to 2 inches wide.

3. Hot Crossed Buns (5.6)
Smear up and right on the first moves leading to knobs and easier climbing. A crack near the top takes small protection. This pitch shares anchor bolts with Biscuit and Gravy.

4. Biscuit and Gravy (5.8)
Beware the low crux and a potentially rough landing; the belayer should spot the leader until the first bolt. Then ascend right to a 5.6 crack that takes small gear (cams .5 inches to 1.25 inches), or veer left up an unprotected 5.6 face. Easier climbing awaits above.

5. Mere Image (5.7)
This pitch meanders left and right over a prominent white dike. While the climbing is great, the runout is unnerving; don't make this your first 5.7 lead. Cracks along the way take cams from .5 inches to 1 inch wide.

Descent
Rappel from the anchors using two 60-meter ropes.

Bunny Slopes (5.6-5.9)

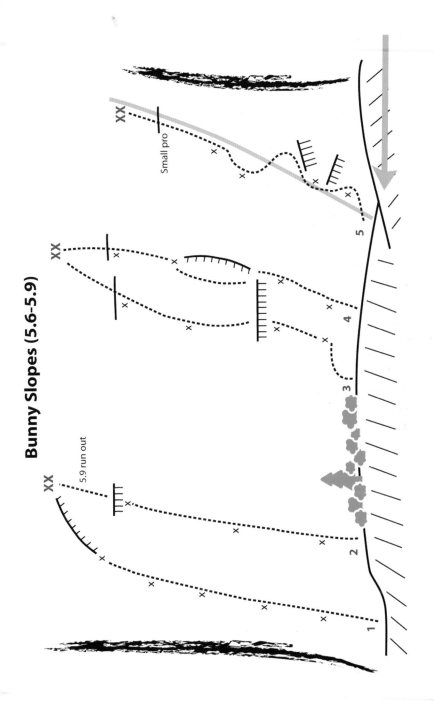

Small pro

5.9 run out

Daff Dome: Guide Cracks

Area: Tuolumne Meadows
Difficulty: 5.5 to 5.8
Parking: beside Tioga Road at Daff Dome
Best season: May through October

Overview

Easy cracks make this an excellent place to start leading on gear. Two bolted anchors protect four pitches known as the Guide Cracks, each about 70 feet long.

Skills needed

Climbers will need to tie into a rope, lead pitches rated from 5.5 to 5.8 while placing gear, belay lead pitches, and build an anchor with bolts.

Gear needed

Take helmets, harnesses, shoes, belay devices, locking carabiners, six quickdraws, a set of nuts, cams from .5 to 3 inches wide, and a rope 50 meters long or longer.

Approach

Park beside Tioga Road at Daff Dome, 3 miles east of Tenaya Lake or 3.5 miles west of the Tuolumne store. Hike north on the southeast flank of the dome, following a use trail beneath trees for about 10 minutes.

1. Lieback Jack (5.8)

Climb the 5.8 lieback to the top of the pillar. Then ascend the crack and a slab to anchor bolts on the right. If the lieback gives you pause, you could lead Is Eight Enough? to the bolts and top-rope this pitch.

2. Is Eight Enough? (5.8)

Jam your fingers, hands, and toes into the 5.8 crack that starts this pitch. Above, a right-facing dihedral leads to a slab and anchor bolts the pitch shares with Lieback Jack.

3. Lucky Seven (5.7)

Count yourself lucky to climb this pitch, because Yosemite doesn't have many short 5.7s. A nice crack leads to a sloped ledge and anchor bolts shared with Welcome To The Club.

4. Welcome To The Club (5.5)

The easiest of the Guide Cracks, this is where many first-timers join the ranks of Yosemite leaders.

Descent

Lower climbers from the anchors or rappel.

Insider tips

Most climbers use a small number of medium-sized nuts and cams; a giant rack of gear should not be needed.

To beat crowds, climb early or late in the day, especially on weekends.

El Capitan: Pine Line

Area: Yosemite Valley
Difficulty: 5.7
Parking: beside Northside Drive at El Capitan
Best season: all year

Overview

El Capitan beckons the world's best climbers but you don't have to be an expert to start on The Captain. The first pitch of The Nose features a fun finger crack and a wonderful view.

Skills needed

Climbers will need to tie into a rope, lead a 5.7 pitch, build an anchor using a tree, belay a lead pitch, and rappel.

Gear needed

Take helmets, harnesses, shoes, belay devices, locking carabiners, six quickdraws, a few long slings, a set of nuts, cams from .25 inches to 2 inches wide, and a rope 50 meters long or longer.

Approach

Pick up the trail leading from the road north toward El Cap. Follow it for a few hundred yards until reaching a dirt clearing. Take the use trail leading left and look on your right for a ledge that rises above most of the trees. Scramble up its left (west) side until you see the crack. The Nose is El Cap's southernmost profile and should be the first formation you see when hiking from the road.

Pine Line (5.7)

Enjoy looking at 3,000 feet of vertical granite above you as you scale this climb. From the beginning, the pitch is a stiff 5.7; placing a few pieces early is a good idea. This crack takes nuts well. Cams will be helpful but not necessary. A pine tree on the ledge provides the anchor. Leave a sling if needed.

Descent

Rappel from the pine tree.

Insider tips

This sunny spot gets hot in summer; start early or late to beat the heat.

After anchoring to the pine tree, climbers can top-rope face climb right of the crack.

Low clouds envelop El Capitan.
Photo by Jeff Vendsel.

Sunnyside Bench: Regular Route

Area: Yosemite Valley
Difficulty: 5.4
Parking: beside Northside Drive near Yosemite Falls
Best season: all year

Overview

Crack, face, and chimney climbing skills come into play on three pitches near Yosemite Falls. This climb provides a comfortable and rewarding first multipitch lead.

Base of Sunnyside Bench: Regular Route

Skills needed

Climbers will need to tie into a rope, build anchors using a tree and gear, lead pitches up to 5.4, and belay a lead.

Gear needed

Take helmets, harnesses, shoes, belay devices, locking carabiners, long slings, six quickdraws, a set of nuts, cams from .5 inches to 3 inches wide, and a rope at least 50 meters long.

Approach

Take the paved trail to the Lower Yosemite Falls viewing area. Cross the bridge and hike 50 yards east. Cut left (north) off the trail and uphill toward a gully. Climb the gully to a tree and the base of a chimney.

Regular Route (5.4)

Pitch 1: A chimney leads to a crack on the left. Use the tree above for the anchor.

Pitch 2: Step out onto the ledge to the right (east) to find cracks leading up and right. The pitch ascends ledges and boulder-like problems to another large tree, which provides the next anchor.

Pitch 3: Avoid a tempting wrong turn up a gully to the left. Instead, traverse right and up on 5.4 holds to a horizontal crack, or climb straight up a vertical crack (5.5) before traversing right to the horizontal crack. Follow it right and then ascend a more vertical crack to a ledge. Build your last anchor.

Descent

Hike uphill a few hundred feet to a use trail. Hike east for about a quarter mile until you see stables and a maintenance yard below. Scramble to the valley floor and hike west to return to Northside Drive.

Insider tips

Before descending, enjoy a close-up look at the waterfall.

Avoid rappelling down the route; there may be climbers beneath.

Sunnyside Bench: Regular Route (5.4)

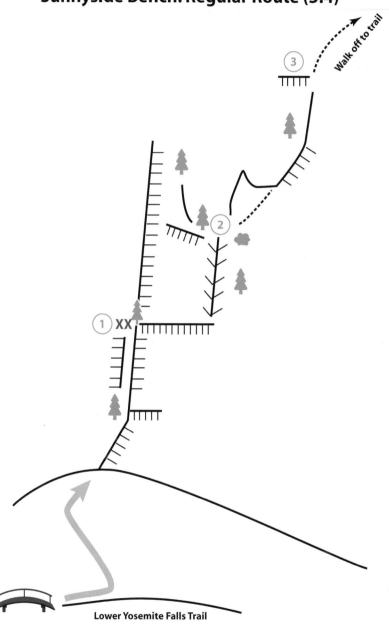

Walk off to trail

Lower Yosemite Falls Trail

Pywiack Dome: Zee Tree

Area: Tuolumne Meadows
Difficulty: 5.7
Parking: beside Tioga Road at Pywiack Dome
Best season: May through October

Overview

Well-bolted 5.7 slab climbing leads to easier pitches above. The upper pitches need gear and the last involves a 5.7 lieback.

Skills needed

Climbers will need to tie into a rope, build anchors using bolts and gear, lead pitches up to 5.7, belay lead pitches, and rappel.

Gear needed

Take helmets, harnesses, shoes, belay devices, locking carabiners, long slings, 12 quickdraws, a set of nuts, cams from .5 inches to 4 inches wide, and a 60-meter rope (a second 60-meter rope will be needed to rappel from belay stations).

Approach

Park beside Tioga Road at Pywiack Dome, either 1 mile east of Tenaya Lake or about 6 miles west of the Tuolumne store. Scramble down talus, cross the stream bed, and hike up the low-angle base. The route starts right of the dikes and beneath a small pine tree. Walk up a class 4 slope to anchor bolts at the base.

Zee Tree (5.7)

Pitch 1: Climb up 5.7 slabs past the tree to the next belay above a small ledge.

Pitch 2: This easier and shorter pitch has three bolts on 5.0 climbing.

Pitch 3: Continue to a crack system where small gear is needed to build an anchor.

Pitch 4: Follow the crack to its top. Build another anchor.

Pitch 5: Traverse to the left and build an anchor beneath the vertical crack.

Pitch 6: Use large cams to protect the 5.7 lieback on the final pitch.

Descent

Hike to the summit and then northeast to find a block with slings. Rappel from it 40 feet and then walk north about 100 feet. Scramble down the talus to the base.

Insider tips

If rappelling, do so after the first or second pitch. After that, rappelling requires leaving gear.

The fourth and fifth pitches can be combined; use long slings to prevent rope drag.

Pywiack Dome: Zee Tree (5.7)

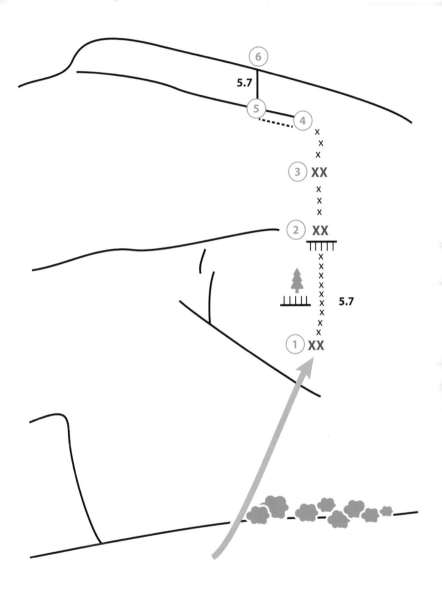

Half Dome: Snake Dike

Area: Yosemite Valley
Difficulty: 5.7
Parking: Curry Village
Best season: June through October

Overview

This classic provides a moderate climb up Half Dome, the most coveted summit in Yosemite. The length of the route, its approach, and descent make for a hard but rewarding adventure.

Skills needed

Climbers will need to tie into a rope, build anchors using bolts, lead pitches up to 5.7 with bolts and gear, belay lead pitches, and rappel.

Gear needed

Take helmets, harnesses, shoes, belay devices, locking carabiners, long slings, six quickdraws, a set of nuts, cams from .25 inches to .75 inches wide, and a 60-meter rope.

Approach

To start from Yosemite Valley, park at Curry Village. Take the shuttle or walk to Happy Isles. From here to the base of the climb is 6 tough miles, gaining 2,500 feet and taking 3 or 4 hours, hence the journey's nickname, "Snake Hike." Starting before dawn is a good idea.

Take the Mist Trail past Vernal Fall toward Nevada Fall (see map on page 87). After about 3 miles, you will reach a trail junction beneath Liberty Cap. Turn left onto the John Muir Trail for a half mile. Just before the next junction, look for a use trail leading north over the ridge that's east of Liberty Cap. At first, it should be steep, bushy, and marked by stacked stones. Follow it for about a mile through the woods and past Lost Lake until you climb up bushy talus to the southeast base of Half Dome. Continue to the west up more talus and slabs. When you can look down on a plateau to the southwest, the route should be directly above on your right.

Snake Dike (5.7)

Pitch 1: Climb to the right of the roof to place gear, which protects the traverse left across polished granite. When climbing over the roof, it's better not to place gear to avoid rope drag.

Pitch 2: Traverse right about 20 feet and then over the roof. Climb up the dike to the anchor bolts.

Pitch 3: Resist the urge to follow the dike further right. Instead traverse left, smearing on friction. One bolt protects the crux. When you reach the vertical dike, skip another bolt on its left (to avoid rope drag) before climbing up 5.4 features to the next anchor bolts. Get used to long runouts!

Pitch 4: Don't miss the bolt on the right halfway up the 5.4 pitch; it's the only protection until the anchor bolts.

Pitch 5: Take the right fork of the dike leading to a crack which takes small gear. There's no protection on the 5.3 dike above until the anchor bolts.

Pitch 6: Follow the 5.3 dike for about 100 feet. A bolt protects the steeper upper portion where a crack leads to the next anchor bolts.

Pitch 7: Climb up the 5.2 face to a seam and then a ledge. Build an anchor with gear.

Pitch 8: Climb the ramp up to right and then traverse left across a face over an easy roof.

Descent

From the last pitch to the top of Half Dome is a hard walk up class 3 and class 4 slabs of 30 minutes or more.

The return to Happy Isles is 8.2 miles. Descend down the steel cables on Half Dome's northeast slope where many now wear harnesses and clip in for safety. Then hike to the first John Muir Trail junction and turn right toward Yosemite Valley. This will take you all the way to Happy Isles. You could also turn right onto the Mist Trail above Nevada Falls for a shorter but steeper trip.

Insider tips

Take gloves to wear when descending the Half Dome cables.

Do not count on getting water from Lost Lake, which is often a muddy marsh.

Treat yourself to a nice dinner after this hard and glorious day!

Half Dome: Snake Dike (5.7)

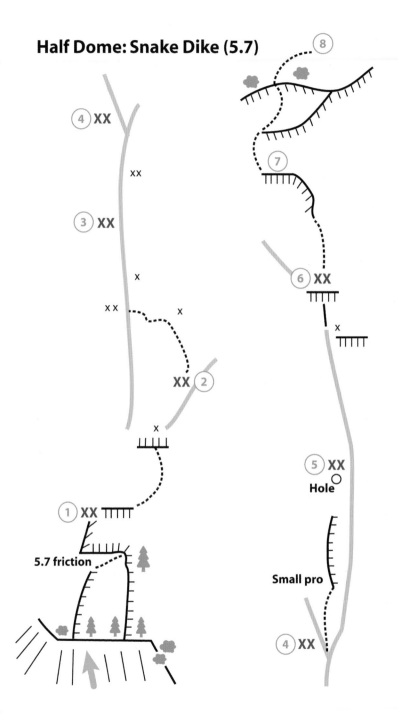

4 XX

XX

3 XX

X

X X

X

XX 2

X

1 XX

5.7 friction

8

7

6 XX

X

5 XX
Hole

Small pro

4 XX

Acknowledgments

In Yosemite I learned that a climber gets nowhere without a good partner. I'm lucky to have many who have "belayed" me in this effort and others.

For supporting and encouraging my writing in recent years, I'm grateful to Niels Aaboe, Kristin Bender, Cathy Claesson, Bob Evans, Frank-Deiter Freiling, Kristina Hacker, Bob Lorentzen, Matt Niswonger, Emily Schult, Mark Slider, Ian Stewart, and the International Center for Journalists.

Thanks to those who shared their time and expertise, making this book far better than it would have been without them. Morry Angell created the rock climbing graphics, Hans Florine wrote the foreword, Bill Gracie proofread the manuscript, Dan Johanson shot the cover photo and other images, Barry Parr, Chris McNamara, and Matt Jacobs advised and assisted me on map production, Adam Schneider and gpsvisualizer.com made the elevation profiles possible, Jeffrey Trust of the National Park Service helped to fact check, Jeff Vendsel helped edit the photos, and Howard Weamer shared his matchless backcountry skiing knowledge.

Extra credit goes to these sharp-eyed proofreaders from *The Olympian* Media Empire of Castro Valley High School: Cameron Beresini, Robbie Brandt, Lily Carrell, Kelly Chan, Eva Chen, Alison Dhont, Rachel Du, Stephanie Huerta, Lauren Jelks, Reema Kakaday, Evan Kwong, Joyce Liang, Sally Liang, Jamie Logan, Tyler Macias, Felicianna Marquez, Grace Moon, Anna Nguyen, Amelia Ortiz, Kate Pellegrini, Tyler Quan, Amanat Riar, Brittany Roberts, Callie Ross-Smith, Leia Saelee, Anna Talajkowski, Matt Talajkowski, Audrey Vandiver, Olivia Wallace, and Daniel Witte.

Noah Amstadter, Don Gulbrandsen, and Jesse Jordan at Triumph Books believed in this project and helped me bring it to life, fulfilling a dream that dates back 20 years. I appreciate it.

Heartfelt thanks go to close friends and relatives who have shared many outdoor adventures with me, including Morry Angell, Bill Bailey, Paul Denzler, Richard DeYoung, Keith Doran, John Dunphy, Linnae Johansson, Peter Johansson, Raffi Kevorkian, Bob Leung, Andy Padlo, Anna Padlo, Lynn Padlo, Zach Padlo, and Steve Schneider. I'm especially grateful to Cliff DeYoung, who introduced me to Yosemite and taught me to climb.

Finally, I'm very fortunate to have a wonderful family that supports me in everything I do. More thanks and love go to my wife, Karen Johanson; my parents, Tom and Diane Johanson; Dan and Hazel Johanson and their children, Nathan and Kaitlyn; and Steve and Galina Johanson and their children, Tommy and Sophia.